The Man in Management

The Man in Management

A Manual for Managers

LYNDE C. STECKLE, Ph. D.

Partner,
William, Lynde and Williams, Psychological Consultants
to Management, Painesville, Ohio

ILLUSTRATIONS BY DOROTHY LESSER

HARPER & BROTHERS · PUBLISHERS · NEW YORK

Library of Congress catalog card number: 58-6138

It took a long time to make a man. Records preserved as fossils indicate that more than five hundred million years elapsed between the appearance of the first recognizable organisms and that of the animal the anthropologists are willing to call a man, that is, a member of the genus Homo. Our species, Homo sapiens, the wise man, has been around for several hundred thousand years. He was not very wise at the beginning, but in due time he did learn to talk, to use fire, and to invent useful tools. The learning process has been going on continuously and at an accelerated rate until now, but Homo sapiens is not as wise as he thinks he is. Recently it has become apparent that he failed to learn how some of the fundamental biological principles must be adapted for successful living at his present stage of cultural evolution. His vast accumulation of knowledge has not yet given him the wisdom to keep the peace with himself and with his fellow men. Unless this defect can be remedied, and that right soon, his name may have to be changed to Homo stultus." (C. Herrick, *The Evolution of Human Nature,* Texas University Press, Austin, 1956, p. 9, reproduced by permission.)

Contents

Contents

Preface

This book is an outgrowth of some twenty years of effort in presenting the facts of human nature to college student, supervisor, foreman, manager, and executive. To the members of these various groups I owe whatever effectiveness I may possess in communicating psychological fact to a nonpsychological public. Wherever I fail to so communicate, the fault is mine and it means that I have not learned my lessons well.

For that which may be helpful to others as they may read this book, credit must go to my colleagues in William, Lynde and Williams. These representatives of permissive yet persistent guidance have contributed much more than they may realize. In countless ways they have assisted me to clarify my own thinking and to place checkrein upon the appealing but wild idea. To Drs. W. E. Brown, T. L. Chappell, L. D. Edmonson, W. H. E. Geiger, R. W. Henderson, R. L. Kaiser, and L. E. Saddler I give my deepest appreciation.

Where direct and forthright suggestion be concerned, I must mention the men of management of Chase Brass & Copper Co., Cooper-Bessemer Corp., Diamond Alkali Co., and Thompson Products, Inc. Members of the management of these organizations have been extremely helpful, most so, perhaps, when they have been at their critical worst. To them a hearty: "Thank you, very much indeed."

To all, student, industrialist, and colleague alike with whatever sincerity words are capable of expressing, I am deeply, deeply grateful.

January, 1958

L.C.S.

The Man in Management

Introduction

FOR the past decade men of management, from supervisor to president, have been submerged in a welter of "how to do its" where people are concerned. In your job, you as a manager—whether of a dozen machine operators or a multiplant corporation—have been told in an infinite variety of forms how best to motivate, inspire, and encourage your people. You have had man classified in all the manner of ways that fertile imaginations, glib tongues and pseudoscientific approaches have made possible. You have been told that mankind is divided into introverts and extroverts, into ectomorphs, endomorphs, and mesomorphs, into the deliberative, the volatile, the impulsive, the thoughtful, the sentimental, the objective, the emotional, the rational, the whatnot types. And, for each "type" of person you have been given a formula that was supposed to assist you in making your appeal to the person more effective so that your will should be done. You have bought as many systems for the motivation of man as there have been ingenious minds to dream them up. Small wonder that the curious among you should be asking: "Just what is going on?"

What has been happening has been no more than the ex-

1

pression of our human desire to short-cut and to search for simple remedies. We, you and I, are the principle advocates of the "easy way"; we want so badly to "do it now." As a consequence, whatever seems quick, looks easy, and promises immediate results appeals to our bustling, Americanized souls. We seem not to care whether the practice is based on fact or on fiction—we ask only that it be fast.

In so far as a rational examination of the "how to do its" for the guidance and direction of the man on the job may be indicative, it very much looks as though we subscribe fully to the conviction that any hog will find acorns (if he scurries about madly enough) however blind he may be. We apparently believe that if we wish to reproduce the world's great literature, all we need do is to place a monkey before a typewriter, energize him with an adrenostrychnine solution and let him type! We somehow seem to feel that if we can hit on the right combination of panaceas, we need not be concerned about fundamentals so long as our cure-alls are applied vigorously, continuously, and with an abundant optimism.

At this point we act with much more enthusiasm than skill, and with considerably more hope than knowledge. As we openly say: "Whadda we care about 'why'—just so long as it works!" The real tragedy is that by and large the "it" does not work at all; we get blinded by the verbal magician who plays so expertly upon the simple wishfulness that seems to be our inheritance.

Because we have defined ourselves as rational beings, we assume that we naturally would not be doing it if it were not logical. And, of course, if the program for the motivation of man appeals to *us*, the final criterion is met. For, after all, we *know* people, we can *tell* the difference between the phony and the honest, we can judge character! We neglect to realize that it is upon this precise belief that the confidence man operates so successfully.

The price we pay for this is reflected in the question many a more reflective management man now is asking himself: "What has training done for us?" This is a good and sound question and when answers are sought seriously, they most often are quite embarrassing. And why should this not be so? How may it be possible for programs of training born of expediency and fostered by phonetics to be anything other than sheerly appealing? How is it possible to understand a finished product with no knowledge whatsoever of the materials and operations that went into its making? No man of management—who hoped to survive long—would purchase a machine or a product just because the descriptive brochures "sounded good." Yet, this same management man who abruptly refuses to purchase without investigation and test when he is dealing with the physical materials of his trade, gleefully will impose upon his organization a program of human development and training just because he likes it. When asked why his company is doing this or that in the training area, a man of management very well may reply: "Oh, I don't know—everybody's doing it. There must be some good in it and anyway it can't do any harm." Can it not indeed! How long may "wolf" be cried and still arouse the populace? How long can human motivation be kept at its peak through multiple "shots in the arm"? Just how long, Mr. Manager, can you keep your people fooled?

As with most problems in life there are apparent answers that should not be mistaken for effective solutions. Furthermore, it usually is easy to do the expedient thing but not always so easy to do the job right. As you very well know (if you will think for a moment), those programs most solidly based upon research and development in both the product and the market areas are most likely to be profitable. If you wish your solution to the "people problem" to be a profitable one, would it similarly not be advisable to base this solution upon a careful study of the facts as they are known to exist? Does it not make sheer common sense to know what your product can do within the market available for it before you begin production? If, where people are concerned, your product is productivity, should you not tailor your operations designed to obtain productivity to those best adapted to utilize the maximum potential that your "equipment" has to offer? If you must work with and through man, should you not know the kind of stuff of which man and his behavior is made that you may better mold and shape it? If you know what man actually is, how he got this way and what, therefore, you best can do about it, are you not in a better position to make your treatment of him oriented toward the productivity you wish?

When you consider that human attitudes, feelings, and general unhappiness cost American industry over 3 billions of dollars every year, you realize that real values are involved. Right in your organization, one-quarter of your working force is sufficiently disturbed emotionally that it adds its contribution to these lost billions through illness, accident, spoilage, resentment, absenteeism, and sheer: "Don't do any more than you have to for the so and so's." [1]

With training that is based upon the factual knowledge man has gained about himself, you have a chance to reduce the degree to which these human failings are cutting into your profit picture. Sensible practices born of realistic information about man's make-up can increase the probabilities that your organization will grow in human productivity. But, there are no panaceas, there are no magic incantations, there are no mystic formulas that can guarantee quick success—there is only knowledge and effort. This is the slow way and if you are interested only in fast answers, read no farther—there will be

[1] "Tension and the nerves of the nation—Psychiatry Eyes the Breaking Point," *Newsweek*, March 5, 1956.

nothing in this book that can help you. However, if you are willing to broaden your knowledge of man and to develop the tolerance and patience that may grow from your increased understanding, then you have a chance of being helped. Since, however, there are no guarantees of success when we humans attempt to influence the behavior of our fellow men, you will have to settle for only a better-than-average bet.

As you very well know, the variations in patterns of human behavior are tremendous. In fact, people vary so greatly, one from another, that often only a buzzing confusion develops in the mind of the man who tries to "understand" them. The facts of such variance account for the appeal of the simple program that classifies human behavior into a few mutually distinctive categories and thereby "simplifies" the problem. That the classification contains but the most superficial knowledge or, in many cases, is not even true, does not disturb because it is so obviously something that can be done to people. We shall see that very little can be done *to* people in our culture, but that a very great deal may be done *with* them.

Our task will be one of boiling down human behavior into its essence, of reducing human behavior to its least common denominator, of describing man as he is rather than verbalizing about what he *ought* to be. In this effort we shall have very little to say about the infinite ways in which human behavior varies; we are not going to talk about individual differences but we shall have a lot to say about individual similarities. Our point of departure will center about the basic, biological nature of man, about those aspects of man's make-up that all of us share, about the structures and functions that are common to you and to me. The assumption is that when we understand how we got to be what we are, we are in a position more adequately to realize why we behave as we do. Knowing these things, we arrive at the point where we have a chance of doing something about it.

Perspective

WHEN the demands of our job present problems that are new to us, problems that neither our past experience nor our routine behavior can answer readily, we at once begin to search about for information that bears upon this new task. We look for this knowledge in several areas. We may tap into the experience of others by talking to those people who have been through this before and who therefore are in a position to help. We may go to the technical literature to find out what has been done in the past. We may look through manufacturers' brochures. We may "think" about the problem, scrambling through all the things that have happened to us as we try to find similarities or analogies that may bear upon the current issue. In whatever we do, one central theme is apparent: we are trying to get the history of the task because we know that once we grasp what has gone before, we are in a much better position to deal with the "what is now." Boiled down, we are looking for perspective.

In the light of this standard practice upon which we fall back when we are faced with novel demands, would it not be intelligent as we pose the "problem" of man, once again to look for perspective? Should we not dig into man's history on the assumption that once we understand how man developed, we arrive at a viewpoint from which his present behavior may make more sense to us? When we know how we got this way, we are in a position to understand the ways into which we have gotten.

As we attempt to move in on man's history, we need to shape our attitudes so that we are most able to accept what we may find. To so prepare ourselves, it becomes most important that we should try to strip away from our thinking our value judgments about man. Value judgments have a habit of beginning with such terms as: "He ought," "He should," "He must," etc. Whenever you have said (as you most certainly have): "He should have known better" you have made a value judgment. You have judged the behavior by a principle that you believe ought to apply; you have reflected in your judgment a value that man has imposed upon himself. So long as you do this, you are in no position to understand human behavior, you are in a position only to criticize and to second guess it. Value judgments, by and large, are ideals toward which we say man should strive. This is fine and, in view of our cultural documents this is "right." But when we attempt to identify an ideal with an actuality, we make a heap of trouble for ourselves.

If you look back into your life experience, you will find, I believe, that many of the difficulties you have had with your fellow man have occurred because you mistook a value judgment for a fact of human behavior. When we judge our fellows (and Mr. Manager, your job centers largely about precisely such judgments) on the basis of what we believe ought to be true, we place ourselves in a situation more likely to be characterized by heat than by light. When a person does not behave as we believe he should behave then obviously there must be something wrong with him. Our stand right here is that the probabilities indicate that something is wrong with our basis of judgment. Consequently, if we wish for a perspective upon man that is at all realistically based, we must strip away the "should be's" from our thinking as we look for the things that are. Therefore, in our brief tour through the history of man, we are going to examine this history in the light of the facts that can emerge and we shall leave the ideals allocated to their proper role—that of goals toward which man is striving. So, as you read the material to come, try to avoid the feeling: "But it shouldn't be this way" because, my friend, this is the way it is.

We know that man has inhabited this earth for a long, long time. We know that the "naked, erect, and featherless biped with flat nails," we call *Homo* (man) has an ancient although not quite honorable history. This fact we have long suspected. Around 3500 B.C., ancient Sumerians estimated that mankind was 473,000 years old. This is surprisingly close to what we now know to be the case. "True" man goes back just about this far as more recent discoveries of human fossil and artifact attest. In fact, scholars of science tell us that man's technology can be traced back 500,000 years! But this should hardly surprise us. If we find evidence that man worked stone this long ago (and we do find such evidence) then obviously there must have been an application of the principle of the lever, of pressure points, of cleavage planes, and the effect upon physical structures of sudden changes in temperature. Furthermore, way back then man produced his stone tools far in excess of his immediate needs; the probabilities are strong that he "warehoused" them.

However, whether early man was a scientist, a toolmaker, or both is of small matter at the moment. We need only to grant that man's history on earth has been of long duration to begin to see human behavior in realistic perspective. Nor do we need to go back into the hundreds of thousands of years that he has been around; we need only to accept his having been around as a *fact* and we can take off from there.

For the purposes of our discussion, let us go back into human time only so far as to assure ourselves that we are dealing with a person like you and me who happened to live some thousands of years ago. This may not be as easy as it sounds. Human beings, with a terrestrial span of some seventy years, often have great difficulty in conceiving of time beyond their own allotted amount. While it may be typical of the human ego to measure all things in terms of its own standards, we must stretch our imaginations beyond their usual limits if we are to obtain the perspective we seek. Therefore, think about and come to accept the fact that humans, just like you and me, lived and behaved many thousands of years before us. Actually, if the millions and millions of years that have passed since life began on earth were to be compressed into the twenty-four hours of the day, man, as we know him (Homo sapiens), would be shown as appearing only during the last few seconds of this twenty-four hour period. We shall try not to test credulity too strenuously, but we must come to understand the man before us if we hope to comprehend the man of today. In our search for perspective, let us go back through human time no farther than to a member of the human race about whom we know a great deal.

Shortly after the end of our Civil War, an excavation for road-building purposes uncovered the remains of human beings in the Cro-Magnon valley in southern France. Because of the accident of location, we have referred to this human as "Cro-Magnon man." We know a lot about this fellow; at least a hundred complete skeletons have been found. We know that Cro-Magnon man corresponded to the white peoples of today. We know he ran big, that he averaged six feet tall, and that he was exceedingly muscular. We know these things because of what his bones tell us. We can measure the length of the skeleton and thus arrive at the height of the person.

Body muscles leave the marks of their insertions and origins upon the bony structure and from the size and depth of these markings we can know how large the muscle was. While it is a fine art indeed, living tissue can be reconstructed from a dead piece of bone and so from the skeleton, the body can be built. From discoveries made and our knowledge of the various body and racial types existent today, we also know that by the time of Cro-Magnon, at least two other forms of man had emerged. Skeletal remains indicate that both the Negro and the Oriental also were present and man as a species was pretty well determined. This conclusion results from the similarities between these skeletal remains and the bony structure of the present Negro and Oriental. At least three of our present racial types were already living some 25,000 years ago.

We say 25,000 because the Cro-Magnon period extended between 28,000 and 23,000 B.C. After this time biological mergers had occurred often enough so that Cro-Magnon as a distinct type largely had disappeared. However, certain survivals still appear in southern France and especially in the Canary Islands. The natives of these islands are Cro-Magnons with little change. There simply can be no question but that the man we call Cro-Magnon existed. Furthermore, we find additional proof in the fact that we are living today as well as his appearance, in his original form, in certain isolated geographical areas.

However, the fact of existence as such means little for our purposes. What if he did exist? Many manlike forms of life are known to have lived, so what has Cro-Magnon to do with us and our understanding of the man of today? This is the crux of the issue.

Fortunately, we know much more about Cro-Magnon than the information already presented. First of all, we know what he looked like because, given the skull, we can reconstruct the facial features. This is common practice in police laboratories all over the world. Think a moment. Over the face there are at least five reference points where the skin is thin, e.g., the forehead, each cheekbone, the bridge of the nose, and the point of the chin. From these reference points combined with the marks overlying tissue may leave on the underlying bone, it is possible to rebuild the face with surprising accuracy. When this is done in the modern laboratory and the person who owned the skull originally can therefore be identified, comparisons between the reconstruction and photographs taken during his life are highly similar. If we can identify a person through reconstructing his face from the bony structure of the skull, then surely similar methods can tell us what Cro-Magnon looked like. As the reconstruction reproduced in Figure 1 (following page 20) will attest, Cro-Magnon man looked like you and me. He was bigger than most of us and certainly better looking than many. He does not meet the usual expectation of "cave man." Not here do we find the receding forehead, the bulging brows, the heavy chin and brutish appearance that characterizes our stereotype of prehistoric man.

Cro-Magnon man had a brain every bit as large as ours— if not a larger one. A comparison of the two skulls that appear in Figure 2 (following page 20) will give you evidence at this point. Notice that the Cro-Magnon skull is in all ways "typically human." While it admittedly is dangerous practice to reason from brain size to degree of intelligence, the material to follow will show you that Cro-Magnon not only had a big brain, but that he was capable of utilizing the unquestioned potential that resided within it.

In fact, anthropologists and biologists tell us that if a Cro-Magnon infant were to be born into our culture right now, he would meet the demands of present-day living every bit as well as we do ourselves. Of course, in certain sections of the world, he *does*. This last statement carries consequences. If Cro-Magnon man could meet the present cultural demands as well as the man of today actually does, then there has been very little (if any) change in our biopsychological make-up since Cro-Magnon times. Let us examine this hypothesis.

While the bare bones of early man tell us a great deal about him, we cannot obtain the full savor of him until we also look at some of the products of his mind. We need also to take into account the results of his cerebral activity; we need to look at his aesthetic, industrial, and religious products as well. We want to understand the *whole* Cro-Magnon, not merely to marvel at his physique, that we may be able better to understand his modern counterparts. Consequently, let us examine the artifacts of Cro-Magnon's culture—those things and functions that his brain conceived.

First, let us consider his tools. He manufactured both tools and weapons. (We already have mentioned that he stored them for future use, if not for trade.) His primary source of material was flint. This is a very hard rock that has dominant cleavage planes and can be worked into a knife-sharp edge. Studies show us how he worked this material. We know that he developed a "hammer and anvil" technique, that he knew about "strikers" and how to hit a piece of flint so that cleavage occurred along a natural plane and that he was aware of the chipping action that takes place when cold water is skillfully dropped on hot stone. Parenthetically, some writers credit the discovery of the "use" of fire as one of mankind's greatest "inventions." There can be no question but that this early man produced work in stone that created tools of an order high in efficiency as well as in aesthetic appeal. Figure 3 (following page 20) demonstrates some of his stone tools.

Cro-Magnon man also created in bone. He made needles

with eyes, pins, buttons, awls, harpoons, hooks, and all manner of implements both for domestic use and for the chase. Furthermore, these creations went beyond sheer utility and display an awareness of form and beauty that could only have come from a sensitive and able intellect. Some of these practical *objets d'art* appear in Figure 4 (following page 20).

Perhaps the best evidence for the high degree of intellectual ability Cro-Magnon man possessed is to be found in his artistic productions. These, in both paintings and sculptures, range from crude, straight-line drawings, through polychrome, anatomically accurate paintings of the creatures of his time. Furthermore, these latter creations were done in curvilinear perspective that is demonstrable of an ability that only those of us who have not tried to make such drawings will fail to appreciate. Moreover, as time went by, these paintings took on an increasingly "abstract" form until what had been a genuine reproduction of animal form now began but to *symbolize* it. We can see that the symbolic expression of a concept is by no means a modern development. In Figures 5 and 6 (following page 20) we see something of the skill in reproduction that Cro-Magnon man possessed as well as some of his symbolism. The "Venus" (symbolic of a fertility cult?) illustrates the latter and indicates the ability for abstract thinking that we often feel is limited to the man of today.

In cave paintings discovered in Spain, we can see portrayals of men using the bow and arrow. This was indeed one of man's great inventions. How he may have hit upon this idea appears to be unknown. The concept of the bow seems to be one of those apparently simple things whose deceptiveness probably resides in the fact that the tool of the bow and the arrow has been around for so long. We, as children, made them and because of this we take the bow for granted. Yet, it is manifestly improbable that the idea behind this tool could have sprung full-blown from the brow of some neolithic genius. Certainly, the primeval designer must have gotten his idea from some similarity in nature, but just what this may have been we do not know. However, the fact remains that the cave man had the bow and his paintings demonstrate that he knew how to use it. From all that presently can be determined, the development of this weapon alone is ample evidence of the ability to imagine, to think, and to conceive on as high a plane as is possible for man to do today.

We also know that the spear thrower (an extension tool that gave increased force to the cast), the sling, and the bola had been invented, the fat-and-wick lamp, the paint brush, carving tools, musical pipes and flutes, the dressing of hides and their utilization for body coverings (stitched together and made to conform to the body contours), wooden traps for capturing his food animals, sickles—all had been developed and heaven only knows what implements are yet to be discovered. Technology like this can hardly be held to be the products of a subhuman mind. Moreover, experts tell us that spoken and probably written language existed.

In man's development, there have been three giant steps. The first of these involved learning how to use fire, tools, and language. This step Cro-Magnon and his peers took for us. The next one was made some 20,000 years later when we learned how to raise food efficiently and this step dragged behind it the working of metals, the wheel, the plow, the loom, and much of what we refer to as our "technology." The third step is being taken right now and it covers the development of power from heat and the scientific method. Of the two steps taken and the one in process, Cro-Magnon certainly contributed his share.

In point of fact, human needs have not changed since Cro-Magnon times although the answers to these needs have changed tremendously. Look at the comparisons that appear below:

Cro-Magnon Needs	Modern Answers
A tool to obtain food	Food producing and packaging
A tool to kill enemies	Neucleonics
Clothing that lasts	Plastic textiles
A cave that is:	
Warm in winter	Central heating
Cool in summer	Central airconditioning
Some way to combat evil spirits	Education
Some way to heal wounds and cure ills	Medicine
Some way to assure body comforts	Production techniques
Some way to get people to behave	Religion
Protection in case they do not	Organized society

Beyond these, we have evidence to indicate not only the inventive but also the social and religious intellect. Remains indicate that Cro-Magnon man worked together, at least in small groups. We believe that he had a society broken down at a minimum into hunters, artists, medicine men, and priests. He buried his dead and the fact that weapons, tools, food, and jewelry were interred with the body indicates some kind of thought given to a life after death. The existence of some kind of a "death cult" cannot be questioned. Furthermore, the instances of skeletons in which a bone had been broken, had been set and had mended tells us that Cro-Magnon knew something about the reduction of fractures and the immobilizing of the limb until healing had occurred. He also trepanned the living skull, perhaps to let "evil spirits" out for the relief of chronic headache or even, perhaps, to relieve subcranial pressures. For the ultimate in modern touches, we know that he was afflicted by arthritis, but there is no evidence to show that he used the venom from the cobra or the acid from ants to treat it. Probably he was ignorant of medications, except for simple herbals, but in general, he faced and solved the problems that life posed for him. Cro-Magnon was *Homo sapiens* and the functions of his brain did not differ from those cerebral functions that have been characteristic of man historically and remain true today.

The point is that if we can come to understand how it could be true that 25,000 years ago there lived a man equal to us in potential, we will have taken the first step toward understanding the man of today. That such was the case, that Cro-Magnon man was at least modern man's equal in the ability to think, has been stated abundantly. Biologists tell us that *there has been no significant change in man's biological make-up for at least 25,000 years* and it probably has been much longer than this. Furthermore, in *The Columbia Encyclopedia* we find the flat statement that "In both physical and intellectual characteristics, Cro-Magnon man was modern man's *superior*." This is yet worse! Whether or not Cro-Magnon was superior is an academic question but it is vital that we try to understand how he could have been our equal.[1]

Yet, if we stop to think a bit, 25,000 years of human time is not very much for man to have remained relatively stationary in his biological development. Significant biological

---

[1] The question is sometimes asked: "Why, if man has had this great ability for so long, isn't he farther ahead than he now finds himself?" The answer to this can be found in the fact that while man's history has seen the scaling of tremendous heights, it also has descended into the deepest of valleys. A few illustrations: From A.D. 100 to about A.D. 400 it was commonplace for men living in what is now England to have central heating and central plumbing within their homes. Then Roman Britain fell before less cultured but more aggressive people and these centralized conveniences did not reappear for over 1000 years. In the seventh century after Christ, the great library of Alexandria was destroyed by Arabs on the assumption: "If it is in the Koran, it is unnecessary; if it is not in the Koran, it is heresy." Furthermore, during the Dark Ages of western Europe (500-1500) certainly any man born who was intelligent enough to think deeply also realized that if he used his head, he very likely would lose it!

changes occur with an exceeding slowness. Naturally, such changes do not refer to things like the gradual loss of body hair, of wisdom teeth, or of little toes. Significant biological change refers to the kind of differentiation that with relative suddenness would evolve a different type of organism. When nature does a job like this, a tremendous amount of time and a great deal of trial and error is involved. Nature, unlike man, does not try to do big things fast.

Consider for a moment. You are familiar with what man has done to the naturally dark brown mink. Through selective breeding, the mink has now been made to appear in a wide variety of colorations. We can buy its skin in blue, in yellow, in white, in black, in tan, and in most shades in between. Just for the sake of illustration, how long do you think it would have taken the mink, under natural conditions to have evolved himself into, say, the silver-blue variety? Of course, the probabilities all are against such an occurrence taking place in nature unless this new coloration were of marked advantage for the organism. But, suppose it could have happened. Would we be thinking in terms of tens of years, of hundreds of years, of thousands or of tens and hundreds of thousands? Now no one can *know* what this answer might actually be but this question was asked of a couple of scientists who have spent the last two decades in biological research. Their answer, after a great deal of prodding was: "Oh, 25,000 years, at least!" The point is this. If it would take the mink, who breeds seven times more rapidly than man, 25,000 years to effect a significant biological change, then the same period of time is extremely brief for such a change to occur in man. So, you see, credulity is not tested so severely after all.

There are consequences to the conclusion that Cro-Magnon man had the same biological make-up that characterizes the man of today. If it is true that Cro-Magnon and modern man biologically are the same, it follows that such changes as may have occurred have been technological only. Let us see what the implications may be for a creature who is facing the complex and demanding issues of today with a Stone Age biology.

READINGS

Berrill, N., *Man's Emerging Mind*, Dodd, Mead, 1955.
Howells, W., *Mankind So Far*, Doubleday, 1944.
LaBarre, W., *The Human Animal*, University of Chicago Press, 1954.
Luquet, G. H., *The Art and Religion of Fossil Man*, Oxford, 1930.
Osborn, H., *Men of the Old Stone Age*, Scribner's, 1916.
Peake, H. and Fleure, H., *Hunters and Artists*, Yale University Press, 1927.
Senet, A., *Man in Search of His Ancestors*, McGraw-Hill, 1955.
Singer, C. (ed.), *A History of Technology*, Oxford, 1955.
Stewart, G., *Man: An Autobiography*, Random House, 1946.
Wendt, H., *In Search of Adam*, Houghton Mifflin, 1953.

Cave Versus Ranch House

THE fact that Cro-Magnon man and you and I are made of the same stuff becomes vitally important for our understanding of human nature. Even though we carry about the same old body, we cannot question the fact that living conditions have changed tremendously. Let us telescope time a little and imaginatively go back to the days of Cro-Magnon man.

Cro-Magnon man lived under the law of the jungle. The principle of the fang and the claw prevailed, survival went to the quick and the strong, and it was sheerly a survival of the fittest situation. One cannot be certain, of course, but it seems reasonable that it was perhaps a 50-50 bet, when Cro-Magnon man left his cave in the morning on his search for food, whether or not he came back with this food or was himself food in the lair of the sabertooth, the great lion, the dire wolf, the short-snouted bear, the cave hyena, or any other four-footed predator with which he was in competition just to stay alive.

In any case, the problem of obtaining sufficient food to maintain body energy involved struggle and a kind of hand-to-hand conflict.

If Cro-Magnon wanted to eat, he had to find the potential food and then kill it himself. This was not without danger. We know that he ate the wild horse, the bison, the sharp-horned ox, the rhinoceros, the mammoth, and probably anything else that came conveniently to hand. This does not exclude his fellow bipeds. But, whatever he ate, he had to get it himself. There was no calling of the corner grocery with its subsequent rapid delivery.

When Cro-Magnon tackled some of this prospective food, he ran serious personal danger. When he entered into deadly combat with, say, the sharp-horned ox (auroch) he as easily could become impaled upon one of the creature's wickedly-curving horns as he could get his spear into its vital organs. Figure 7 (following page 20) illustrates the possibility. When he hungered for other meats, or chance brought them his way, much the same possibilities prevailed. If he hunted the mammoth, he had to prepare his pit and, once the creature had fallen into it, somehow kill it with stone weapons. This meant close contact with the animal and resistance on the mammoth's part might be expected. If he craved horse meat, he had to run the creature down, drive it over a cliff or in some way to utilize his greater skills to trap or ensnare it. When he went after the bison, he faced the charge of an infuriated ton or more of beef. To meet this, he had only his courage, his spear, his brain, and his agility to sustain him. One can but surmise what the posthunt casualty list commonly may have been. Whatever the actual situation, it certainly was standard operating practice for Cro-Magnon man to fight for his life. As Figure 7 attests, he had to fight for his food and, as you may see from Figures 8 and 9 (following page 20), the competition was terrific! Death by violence was a constant companion.

In large measure early man's hunting was a solitary pursuit or, at best with but a few of his kind. During this era there were probably no more than 100,000 individuals scattered

Figure 1. Cro-Magnon Man.

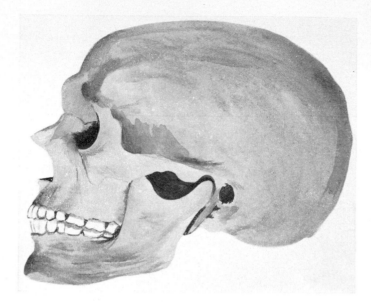

FIGURE 2.   Human Skulls. *Above*, Cro-Magnon Skull;
below, modern skull.

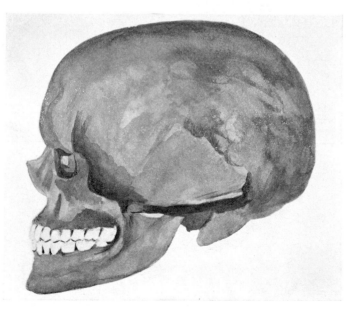

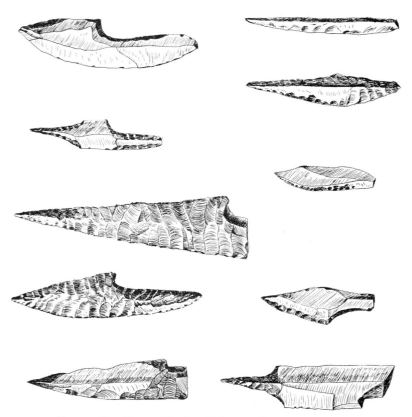

FIGURE 3.   Stone Tools. (After Peake and Fleure.)

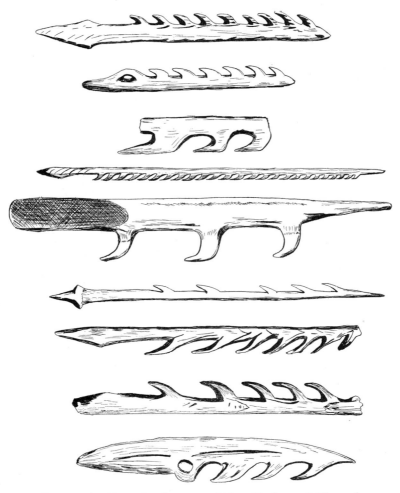

FIGURE 4. Bone Implements. (After Peake and Fleure.)

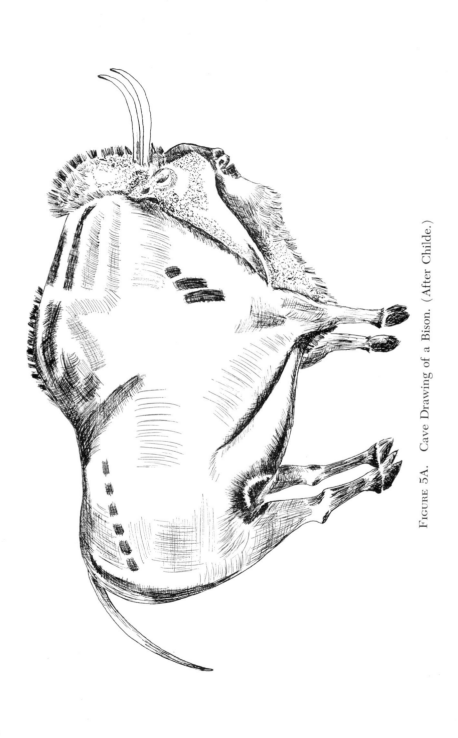

FIGURE 5A.   Cave Drawing of a Bison. (After Childe.)

FIGURE 5B. Cave Drawing of a Reindeer. (After Childe.)

FIGURE 6.   Cro-Magnon "Venus." (After Peake and Fleure.)

FIGURE 7.   The Aurochs Hunt.

FIGURE 8. *Above:* the Dire Wolf, Whose Height at Shoulders is 27 Inches and Average Weight is 175 Pounds. *Below:* the saber-toothed cat, whose height at shoulders is 37 inches and average weight is 400 pounds.

FIGURE 9. *Above:* the Great Lion, Whose Height at Shoulders is 44 Inches and Average Weight is 100 Pounds. *Below:* the short-faced bear, whose height at shoulders is 4 feet and average weight is 2000 pounds.

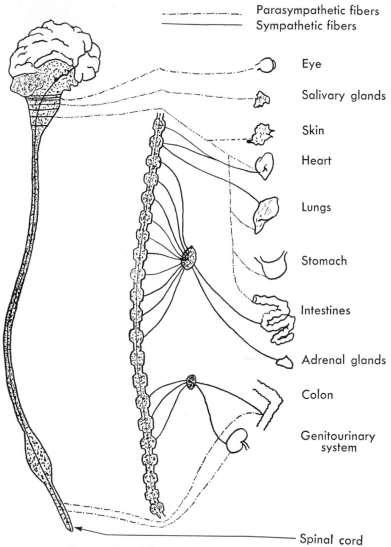

Parasympathetic fibers
Sympathetic fibers

Eye

Salivary glands

Skin

Heart

Lungs

Stomach

Intestines

Adrenal glands

Colon

Genitourinary
system

Spinal cord

FIGURE 10. The Autonomic Nervous System.

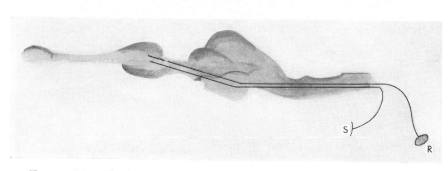

Figure 11.   Shark Brain. This is the most primitive vertebrate brain.

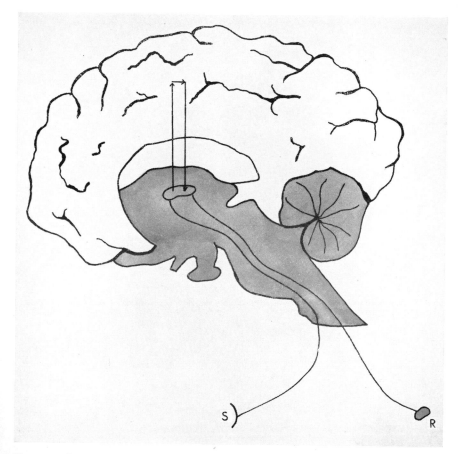

Figure 12.   Human Brain. Shaded area indicates old brain; unshaded area
indicates new brain.

over the area in which they lived. These people were migra-
tory in a small way and they followed the seasons and the
movements of game. They did not stay in any one place for
any lengthy period of time, although they returned over and
over again to "favorite" spots. Most of their groupings involved
three or four families with groups as large as 200 being quite
unusual. This means that except for some special get-togethers
(religious meetings, game or harvest celebrations, or unusually
large numbers of a favored game), Cro-Magnon man traveled
principally alone. He was dependent upon his own know-how,
his own skill and ability, for his livelihood. At best he could
anticipate help from but a few. Although he was not a solitary
animal, he lived right next door to it.

Under such conditions of life, it seems most reasonable that
those Cro-Magnons whose bodies were best adapted for survival under the law of the jungle would tend to survive and
to perpetuate their kind. Contrariwise, those members of the
species whose bodies least well equipped them for such survival simply would get killed off. If this assumption is true
and if there has been no significant biological change in our
make-up since Cro-Magnon times, then it follows that, whatever the mechanism that permitted for this survival may have
been, it still must be present in the body of the man of today.

Let us look into this for a way. We can agree, I believe, that
Cro-Magnon man's life involved rather constant threat. Furthermore, this threat was distinctly physical in nature with
violent and messy dismemberment or death always close at
hand. Suppose we travel back, in our imaginations, to the
southeastern Europe of 25,000 years ago. Suppose you are
a Cro-Magnon. You are walking along a path in a valley.
You have nothing special on your mind; perhaps you are just
out for a stroll. Suddenly you hear a noise. This alerts you
because you have discovered that continuous vigilance is the
price you must pay for your existence. So, you look over your

shoulder in the direction from which the sound apparently came. There above you, set as though to spring, crouches a saber-toothed cat. But, you are a man and you have this big brain of which we humans are so inordinately proud. Consequently, you are not going to make any snap decisions, you aren't going off half-cocked. No indeed, you are a thinking man and you're going to analyze the situation before you act upon it. So, you observe and classify. It appears to you that this cat has at least four knives on each foot and he has four feet; you are armed only with a spear. Furthermore, his teeth obviously are longer and sharper than yours and you suspect that he outweighs you considerably. As a result of this rational analysis, you decide that your only security lies in retreat. Too late! You're a dead Cro-Magnon and before you die you hear your own bones crunch.

Of course, no sensible Cro-Magnon would do anything like this. The probabilities are that even as he perceived the situation he was already setting out to put as much space between the sabertooth and himself as he possibly could. This was no time for thought; this called for action and, without much thinking as such, Cro-Magnon man took it. Within his body there lurked a mechanism designed precisely for just such situations.

You, right now, are no different. Let's test this statement. Suppose you are in Los Angeles where our imaginal situation very easily could occur. Perhaps you are aware from your own experience that in Los Angeles, especially within the suburbs where intersections may not always be guarded by a traffic light, a pair of parallel white lines defines pedestrian passage from one sidewalk to the other. This condition, of course, prevails in most metropolitan areas. However, in Los Angeles there is a difference. This difference consists in the fact that as you step from the curb into the area defined by these lines, oncoming traffic stops. Legally it must do so that you may cross the street in safety. For strangers from our eastern cities, this is a bit of an experience and often develops internal feelings of power as trucks and trailers, sports cars and limousines brake to a standstill just to let them walk across the street. But, if they elect to cross in the middle of the block where these rules do not apply, it's open season and they are on their own.

Let us suppose that you are in Los Angeles and you find yourself in the center of one of these blocks with pressing need (or so it seems to you) to get to the other side of the street. The block is long and, characteristically, you are in a hurry. You look both ways, you don't see anything and so you start across. About halfway over the street you hear a noise and, being also alert because you know you shouldn't be doing this, you look to see what caused it. Instantly, even as you look, you see an automobile bearing down upon you and become aware that collision is imminent. Now, if you stop to calculate relative distances, weights, inertias, etc., the next vehicle to arrive will be white, with little red crosses painted on its sides. Of course you don't think; you get out of there! Perhaps your knees are skinned, your nose bleeding and your heart palpitating, but you are safe. Furthermore, as you look at the distance between where you were and where you now find yourself, you ask: "Who *me?*" You couldn't have leaped that far, but you did! In fact, you behaved exactly as you behaved during your life as Cro-Magnon when the threat was embodied in a sabertooth rather than an automobile. Something happened in both cases, something designed to preserve the body in emergency situations, something took over and protected you, something about which *you* had relatively little to say.

This "something" is the body mechanism to which we have been referring. From these two vicarious experiences, you have perceived it in action. It should be apparent that this mechanism underwrites the preservation of the body in times of stress and this seems to be precisely what it is designed to do. It worked for Cro-Magnon and it still carries out its original function today.

This is what happens. Whenever an organism with a backbone (a vertebrate) perceives threat, certain involuntary, unwilled, and automatic things occur: things over which you have no control. As example, your heart action increases both in rate and force, your blood pressure mounts (sometimes to a startling degree), your breathing changes so that there is more efficient interchange between oxygen and carbon dioxide, the skin capillaries (the little tubes that carry the blood through your skin) constrict, and if you should be cut, you do not bleed as easily as otherwise might be the case. The coagulation time of your blood decreases so that if you do bleed, the blood clots more quickly. Digestion ceases and the blood that has been centering there assisting in the processes of digestion is sent out to the skeletal muscles where the action presumably is to occur. Parenthetically, this happens because digestion is a long-range bet; it is preparing the body for survival tomorrow and the days after. But, when the body is faced with disaster right now, tomorrow and the days to come take on only an academic significance. The problem to be met confronts you now and, if it is not met efficiently, there may be no tomorrows. This your body realizes even if you do not.

In addition to these changes, your liver releases its store of glycogen (blood sugar) into the blood stream and glycogen is the fuel your muscles burn. Your adrenal glands, two little cocked-hat affairs, one perched atop each kidney, pour adrenalin into your blood stream and this is a drug that aids and abets the processes already described. All this occurs in a literal twinkling of an eye and all of it is motivated by just one force—to maintain the integrity of your body when your own carelessness or the stupidity of others has placed you in a situation that may have a fatal termination.

This mechanism underlies and underwrites what we call the "emotions." Having labeled it by its accustomed term, there can be no question in your mind but that it does exist. It becomes important now, after we have identified the process and have discovered what its biological purpose may be, to have a look at its role in our everyday lives, for a role it certainly has.

Let us repeat. This mechanism developed during the eons while manlike creatures and man himself were in the process of adapting themselves to a world that cared little whether or not individual bodies survived. Under the law of the tooth and the talon, the processes of emotion had definite survival value. When this mechanism is activated, it is true that you and I can run faster and farther, we can strike harder and longer, and we can endure more than ordinarily would be possible for us. You may have seen something of the power that is mobilized. You may have witnessed (or even experienced) a man lifting or moving something under emotional stress that was "beyond human strength." An automobile, perhaps, that man cannot lift but, under stress conditions, a man did it! The potential for the mobilization of body energies that lies within us may cause us to gape in openmouthed amazement when we see it in action. There simply can be no doubt but that these forces are present or that it takes an emergency situation to release them.

When you and I or Cro-Magnon man are faced with threat, these forces mobilize for action. For Cro-Magnon there were undoubted advantages to this. Since he had literally to fight for his life as almost a daily experience, the probabilities are that those Cro-Magnons in whom this process ran itself off smoothly would survive. For those whose emergency reactions lagged or were weak, death resulted. The problems of living were straightforward, direct, and immediate. The emotional process was a practical, biological answer to a demanding, biological problem.

In light of the fact that each and every one of us is carrying about a physiological process designed for survival under the law of the jungle, certain interesting questions present themselves. What purpose may this process normally serve today? How commonly are we now threatened with violent and messy dismemberment (the threat the process was designed to meet)? What role may this biological hangover from prehistoric times play in our present lives? What is this physiological atomic bomb doing for (or to) us as we move through our routine affairs? Let us look at some of the answers.

We can observe at once that although our bodies may have undergone no particular change in 25,000 years, enormous things have happened to the conditions under which we live. The contrasts between life in a cave and life in a ranch house are as great as the human mind can imagine. No longer, under the normal conditions of life, are we confronted by need to fight for our very survival; the threat has changed. All of us know that the threat has changed and that it no longer is physical in nature, but psychological. There is no longer a threat to our persons but there is a threat to our personalities. We are not now customarily threatened by dismemberment or death but there is manifold threat to our reputations, our status, our prerogatives, our possessions, our positions, our loyalties, our friends, and our loves. We know that the threat has changed; we know it, but our bodies do not.[1]

[1] For those of you who may be thinking that the automobile constitutes as much threat to our bodies as his four-footed competitors did to Cro-Magnon, a bit of simple arithmetic. Take the number of automotive casualties the National Safety Council predicts for any given year, divide this number by the total population of the U.S. and the resulting fraction represents your individual probability of being killed in an automotive accident. You should get such odds at the race track!

Consequently, it makes no difference to your body whether the threat be a hitherto unseen automobile bearing down upon you or someone saying: "By the way, that female you used to carouse with—you married her, didn't you?" Whatever the perceived threat may be, the subsequent physiological changes occur and, biologically, you are prepared to fight or to run, neither one of which you may conveniently do today. Should you be surprised that energy mobilized for action but that cannot be expressed should create tension within you?

Just to give you some idea of the ramifications involved in these physiological changes that take place under "emotional" conditions, have a look at Figure 10 (following page 20). Notice that from the bottom of the brain fibers (sympathetic, war-time) run out to every bodily organ. (The parasympathetic fibers do also, but since these subserve "peacetime" activity, they are not especially pertinent to our present discussion.) Is it any wonder that when these sympathetic fibers are activated we should experience the "stirred up" condition so common to emotional experience? Let us examine some of the phenomena involved in this physiological relationship and see whether or not we may bring sense into the results of emotional disturbance upon the behavior of the man of today.

READINGS

Childe, V., *Man Makes Himself*, Watts, 1937.
Clark, G., *From Savagery to Civilization*, Cobbett, 1946.
Coon, C., *The Story of Man*, Knopf, 1954.
Henry, T., *"Ice Age Man; The First American,"* National Geographic Magazine, December, 1955.
Hirsh, S., *The Fears Men Live By*, Harper, 1955.
Hoebel, A., *Man in the Primitive World*, McGraw-Hill, Inc., 1949.
Horton, E., *Up from the Apes*, Macmillan, 1946.
Linton, R., *The Tree of Culture*, Knopf, 1955.
Life Magazine, "The Epic of Man," Nov. 7, 1955; Dec. 12, 1955; Feb. 27, 1956; Apr. 16, 1956.
Shapiro, H. (ed.), *Man, Culture and Society*, Oxford, 1956.

Shark and Man

WE HAVE seen that when we (or any organism with a backbone) perceive threat about us, certain physiological things happen to our body quite without decision on our part. We also have seen that the purpose of these changes is to put the body on a war economy, to prepare us for violent and sustained physical action. Furthermore, we have seen that this mechanism served a purpose real and vital for Cro-Magnon man as he faced the threatful realities under which he lived. However, we well may raise the question: "What function may this process serve in our lives today?"

Threat, of course, still is with us—not threat to our lives, but threat to our psychosocial integrity. Nevertheless, our reaction to this threat, physical *or* psychological, biologically is the same; when threat occurs, we become physiologically prepared to fight and the need for solution by combat rapidly has diminished as we have established social institutions to settle interpersonal differences. Consequently, we no longer can find physical release for the energies mobilized by emotional experience and we clearly can see the price we must pay for our very survival. This price results from the fact that a once helpful mechanism now may actually impede interpersonal effectiveness. If it is true that the arousal of emotional activity within us can reduce our efficiency in our dealings with our fellow man, then understanding the fundamentals of this behavior becomes quickly important for you who are in a leadership position. Therefore, we must examine this. Let us see how this mechanism may work against smooth human relations as we go about our daily routine on the job.

Once again we need to look for perspective. Remember, an investigation of what has gone before always is helpful to us (if not essential) as we move into strange problem areas. Faithful to this principle, therefore, let us obtain background on the nature of emotional experience and what it does to us.

In our search for perspective upon this issue, it will be advisable to keep things as simple as possible. Consequently, suppose that we find an organism with a backbone that still lives under the law of the jungle, an organism whose make-up is relatively simple when compared to our own, but one in which the same biological principles apply although in less complex ways. Although several forms of primitive vertebrate life could serve us at this point, let us select the shark. We cannot question the fact that this creature lives under the law of the survival of the fittest, that it must fight just to stay alive and that it is a highly individualistic organism. At least, there is very little evidence to indicate that the shark is noted for its benevolence, consideration, coöperation, or sympathy for the plight of others. In many ways the shark admirably is suited for our purpose.

Suppose, for the moment, that you are a shark. You're swimming along, reasonably content with yourself and at temporary peace with your world, Suddenly, you become aware of an internal disturbance. Your blood sugar level has dropped below a critical minimum and automatically your stomach begins rhythmically to contract. You experience what we humans call "hunger." As a shark, what do you do? You look about yourself, of course, for potential food. If you perceive such, you eat it providing that two, and *only* two, criteria are present: (1) the availability of food, and (2) your ability to capture it.

It makes no difference whatsoever to you if some other individual of your kind has established prior property rights to this bit of food or, if the case should arise, that this bit of food should happen to be your son, daughter, aunt, uncle, mother, father, or aging grandparent. There are, for you, but two questions: "Is food available?" and "Am *I* strong enough to get it?" Only these two factors stand between you and the appeasement of your hunger. Your behavior is immediate, aggressive, and dictated only by your needs of the moment.

Now, let us contrast your behavior as a shark with your behavior as a human being. Suppose you are at momentary loose ends in a strange city. You are in between appointments, trains, planes, or whatever. In any case, you have time on your hands and you are spending it in wandering about the town looking at the buildings, the store windows and, of course (if you are a male), at the girls. Suddenly in the midst of this pleasant perambulating reverie, you too become aware of the same internal disturbance that you have experienced previously during your imaginal existence as a shark. *Your* blood sugar level has dropped and *your* stomach now begins automatically to contract. But you are a man and man can talk. So, you say to yourself: "By golly, I'm hungry. Wait a minute. Back there a block and a half or so there was a restaurant. I'm going to get something to eat." Suiting your action to your words, you turn about and retrace your steps to the restaurant you recall having passed. There, within the customs established by the society in which you live, you appease your hunger pangs.

The important factor in our illustrations of the food-getting behavior in shark and man lies in the *differences* between the ways in which the hunger was met. As a human being, you did not, as your hunger pangs assailed you, seize upon a smaller passer-by and immediately begin to chew upon him. Rather, you inserted a period of *delay* between the time at which you became aware of your hunger and your behavior in responding to it. When you were a shark, no such period of delay intervened if, of course, food were immediately available. In any case, no thoughts about the rights of others, social custom, or cultural expectation entered your behavioral equation, as you, Sir Shark, set about to relieve your hunger. However, in your human form, these factors played a very definite role in determining what your reaction to hunger might be.

At this point, we become interested in the mechanisms behind the variances in behavior we have observed as we study shark and man in a common situation. How may we account for the differences we have seen? To answer this question, let us examine the brain of shark and man to discover whether or not our answers may reside within them.

Suppose we were in tropical waters and we were to catch a shark. After we have it properly subdued and boated, suppose we were to cut open its brain box (skull) and look at the contents. We would discover that the shark has a brain although we might be a little surprised that it should be so small when compared to the size of the creature. But, a brain we would find nevertheless, although this brain will prove to be about as primitive a brain as a vertebrate may possess. We now take this brain out of its cartilaginous box, we properly "fix" it (agglutinate the tissue so that it can be dissected) and we slit it lengthwise, from stem to stern. In Figure 11 (following page 20) we see a diagram of such a section of the brain of the shark.

In this diagram, it is important to notice that the incoming nerves (sensory: "S" in the diagram) go to the great relaying station of the vertebrate brain (thalamus) and that at this point integration occurs and the motor nerves of reaction ("R") immediately are activated. There is little or no delay between the onset of a stimulus and what the shark does about it. Shark behavior is instantaneous, relatively foresightless, and determined by the body needs of the moment. The immediacy of the hook-up between sensory and motor nerves in the shark brain attests to the directness of its behavior that we already have observed. Notice that the shark brain serves only as an integrating organ between incoming and outgoing nervous impulses. The resulting behavior is purely a function of body needs and directed entirely toward the maintenance of bodily integrity. In a sense, we can say that the only thing in which the shark is "interested" is what the shark "wants." Its brain then becomes only a translating device better to assure the creature that these wants are fulfilled.

In contrast, let's take a look at the brain of man. If you will permit it, let us borrow yours. Since our examination will largely be purely imaginal, we shall return it to you undamaged. With your permission then, we open your brain box and we discover that it is not composed of cartilage but of good, solid bone. Within it we see a veritable mass of brain tissue. We remove this brain and this time we are impressed with the size of the organ when it is compared to the size of the body that it governs. We find ourselves in possession of about three pounds of messy substance. This we must again stabilize so that our dissection can be made handily. Once more we slice through this brain as we did with the brain of the shark; we cut it through the middle from stem to stern. When we look at one of the exposed surfaces, we see something akin to the diagram in Figure 12 (following page 20).

Once again we see that a portion of this human brain is greatly remindful of the brain we found in the shark. This primitive brain (old brain), that man possesses along with all other vertebrates, is shaded in our diagram. We observe within it the same identical relationships that we have had occasion to see in the brain of our shark. Once more sensory nerves run to the thalamus and motor nerves run from it; here again we find the great relaying system of the central nervous system as it exists in both shark and man. However, we immediately discover that something has been added. We can see that superimposed upon this old brain there lies a great mass of brain substance. This is the new brain that characterizes the higher vertebrates of which man is one. As we look more closely, we discover that from the primitive relaying station of the thalamus (that alone served as the highest integrating level for the shark) ascending fibers now run up into this new brain and that within its highest level there are associative fibers that connect these ascending nerves with descending ones. Under these conditions, when a message comes to the thalamus from a sense organ, there is now the possibility that before the order for response goes out, the message is relayed upstairs where, in the light of experience, knowledge, and analysis, integration may occur and a behavior pattern ordered that fits both the personal need and the social situation. This "long-circuiting" of the primitive "short-circuit" takes time and it is this period of *delay* made possible (but not, as we shall see, guaranteed) by the new brain that permits behavior we call by such names as "judged," "foresightful," "thoughtful," "considerate," and so on.

Under normal conditions after a life of normal experience, the new brain holds the old brain in check. The autonomy of the old brain that we observed in the shark is denied and its behavior is subject to the dictates of the brain above. However, this occurs under normal conditions and, since life experiences seldom are completely "normal," let us try to find out just how strong this new brain control may be.

An analogy will be helpful at this point. In Figure 13 you will find a "typical" organization chart. In such a diagram a hierarchy of control is implied. You are aware that the man represented by the topmost box holds in check (defines the limits of permissible decision) the behavior of the two men beneath him. Furthermore, these two men similarly "control" the behavior of the men beneath them and so it goes—each level of organization holds in check the behavior of levels

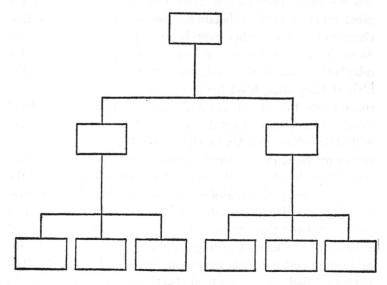

FIGURE 13.

below. Imagine, if you will, that this chart extends all the way down to include the great mass at the bottom composed of the bargaining unit. Ordinarily (under "normal" conditions) the direction of control is from the top down and equally so is this true under normal conditions within the human brain.

A question arises: "Within an organization as diagramed in Figure 13 is it possible for the normal direction of control to be *reversed?*" Of course it is. Think of the thousands of times that so much disturbance has developed at the bottom of the organization (within the bargaining unit) that, for a time, the man on top no longer calls the shots but rather essentially "takes orders" from men beneath him. In fact, let this disturbance become great enough, and the company president jumps through whatever hoop the bargaining unit elects to hold up for him! Our conclusion would be that normally the direction of control within a business organization or a human brain is from the top down, but that when certain unusual (abnormal) conditions prevail, this direction of control may be reversed. This unquestionably is true for the business organization; let us see how this principle may prevail within the brain.

Once again some perspective will be helpful to us. Remember, if you will, the day that your wife came home from the maternity hospital bringing with her that squirming mass of protaplasm—your child. Now think carefully. Was this infant a new brain or an old brain creature? Was its behavior dictated by the consideration-for-others characteristic of new brain function or the insistence-upon-personal-satisfaction that characterizes old brain activity? It was the latter condition that prevailed, was it not? When the infant's colon became full, it "went" did it not? Similarly it made immediate reaction when its bladder filled and all this regardless of time, place, or whose lap it was sitting upon at the time. When its stomach was empty, neither you nor the infant got any rest until it was filled, remember? This immediacy of response to stimulating conditions is typical of old brain operation and we saw this to be true in the case of the shark. The old brain subserves the perpendicular pronoun, the I, and it is concerned only with what the body needs—or feels that it needs. There is no room at this level for the rights and privileges of others; only the self and what it wants are important.

Additional evidence for the "old brainedness" of birth can

be found in the fact that although the adult human brain averages three pounds in weight, at birth the human brain averages but twelve ounces. Furthermore, a child is about six before it is biologically capable of clear distinction between the "I" and the "you" that is so important for easy adjustment to our fellows. Still further, a child is about twelve before its brain takes on the electrical activity that characterizes the adult brain. Parenthetically, you parents might keep this in mind when your four-year-old fails to grasp a typically "adult" concept. When this happens, you will recall, you tend to get angry with the "perversity" of the youngster because of the frustration developed through your own ignorance.

It should be apparent that whatever new brain control an adult may possess has been learned and is not the "natural" state of affairs. If this old brain-new brain relationship is a developed one, then we should like to know something about how long this learning process takes and also something about how well established the lines of control may be.

I am sure that you know a person of 40, 50, or more years of age who still behaves as though his needs, his desires and his wishes were the only important things in the world. His general behavior centers about these feelings and woe betide the unfortunate individual who may stand in the way. Within such a person, the new brain control of the old brain never was very well established and consequently the resulting life behavior largely is "I-centered." This experience illustrates the fact that the development of new brain control is an ongoing process that continues throughout our lives; we never learn it completely. It not only is a relatively recent acquisition in our lives, but it is a state of affairs that we continue to acquire so long as we may live. Keeping the need to consider the other fellow high in our personal equation of life is a task that we work at (normally) all through our earthly existence and also is one that we cannot ever fully achieve; our very biology, our old brain, stands always in the way.

If, therefore, an important life task for each of us centers about the continuous reduction of the weight that the "I" carries in our human equation, we might expect that such new brain control as may be obtained would be rather tenuously established. We might expect that the lines of control would be somewhat weak, rather readily disturbed, and in a state of highly labile equilibrium. This seems to be the case as any of us can discover for ourselves if we wish to put it to the test.

You can check the facts involved when next you attend a cocktail party, if you wish to do so. Remember, however, that there will be a price you must pay in order to do this. Of course, you must always pay a price for any decision that you make. This "price of decision" is often a stumbling block for us humans and we therefore should examine it before we proceed. A very simple illustration will serve: You are out riding on a Sunday afternoon. You're not going anywhere, you're just out for a ride. You come to a fork in the road and, for one reason or another, you decide to turn left. This very decision precludes the possibility of turning right, unless you attempt something very stressful to your auto. From this exceedingly simple situation up to the most important decision you ever may make, the same principle applies. Any decision always will cost you *something*. It therefore becomes important to calculate the price, to ferret out the odds, before you make a decision and, if you are not willing to pay the price involved, then the decision should not be made! Our usual practice, unfortunately (in sound human fashion, by the way), is to make a decision in blind disregard of the price and then, when the price comes due, to complain bitterly and place the "blame" everywhere other than where it rightfully belongs. The fact is that the intelligent person predicts the consequences of the act before he makes it and, if these consequences are those that he does not care to face, he foregoes the act itself. Keep in mind that the decision and its consequent action, in themselves, will very seldom cause you concern, but the price you will have to pay for the decision may disturb you mightily indeed.

But, to return to our cocktail party. If you wish to conduct this experiment, here is what you must do. Connive with your host so that no drinks are served until after all the guests have arrived and there has been opportunity for a few moments of conversation. Get to the party early so that you can watch the others as they arrive and, when the conversation has begun, tap in on it. (We assume that none of the guests have done any closet drinking at home to "get an edge" for the party; we assume that, at this point, everyone is cold sober.) You will find the chitchat running something like this: "How have you been?" "How's the family—the kids doing O.K. in school?" "By the way, the papers told me that you just had a trip. Did you enjoy it? Tell me about it."

Now you wait. You wait for about three cocktails to be served; for the others to consume from four to six ounces of whiskey. And, throughout this waiting, you cannot have even the teensiest drink—if you take just one small one you strongly decrease your ability to make the observations to follow. This is the price you pay, the price of sobriety, and you well may find it a greater cost than you wish to expend.

If, however, you have remained drinkless for the requisite period, you now tap in on the conversation once more. You will discover that some changes have occurred. It now will run something like this: "You think that's somepin? Let me tell you what happened to *me!*" "Look, just keep your mouth shut for a minute and let a man talk who *knows!*" "Man, did *I* have *myself* a time—here's what *I* did!"

The big central factor in the changes you have observed lies in the fact that the direction of behavior has shifted. Originally, you will recall, this behavior was "you-oriented"; the emphasis was upon the other fellow. Now, it has become rather completely "I-centered" and the emphasis is upon the perpendicular pronoun. Interest and stress have moved from the "you" to the "me." It is apparent that the normal control by the new brain has been lessened, that the old brain and its "I-ness" has become dominant. It looks as though the lines of control, established during the life of the people up to this point, have been broken and that the persons involved have retrogressed to a behavior pattern characteristic of their earliest years. What has happened? In the next chapter we will examine some new-brain-old-brain relationships to see what a few ounces of alcohol have done to them.

READINGS

Bosselman, B., *The Troubled Mind*, Ronald, 1953.
Fielding, W., *The Caveman Within Us*, Dutton, 1922.
Hutschnecker, A., *Love and Hate in Human Nature*, Crowell, 1955.
Morgan, J., *How to Keep a Sound Mind*, Macmillan, 1946.
Pfeiffer, J., *The Human Brain*, Harper, 1955.
Selye, H., *The Stress of Life*, McGraw-Hill, 1956.
Steckle, L., *Problems of Human Adjustment*, Harper, 1957.

How Homo *Becomes* Sapiens

HOW does man (*homo*) become wise (*sapiens*)? In most of our cultural documents the broad assumption seems to be made that he is born that way. This we have seen to be untrue. We are born (normally) with the potential for such development, but it takes a lifetime of proper living to approximate the new brain control that most of us take for granted in our dealings with our fellow man. Let us repeat the fact that only in so far as our training and our resulting attitudes align themselves with the principles of democratic living may we possess the kind of interbrain relationships that permit us to become and to remain a member in good standing within our cultural group. The point to be remembered is: "We learn how to keep our new brain (and a consequent "you-orientation") in control and we continue to learn how to do this so long as we may live!"

We already have shown, through our cocktail party experiment, how easily these lines of control may be disrupted. Let us now examine what happens within our brain as alcohol gets into our blood stream.

Despite a lot of conversation to the contrary, alcohol is not a stimulant; it is a depressant as are all narcotics. The reason it seems to stimulate is because it relaxes the very controls we have been discussing and, because you cannot tell how you feel, you think you feel good. Of course, when the morning and its recurring sobriety appear, you *know* how you feel! However, alcohol in the body works like this. Alcohol reduces the ability of nervous tissue to utilize oxygen; the higher the alcohol content of the blood, the less able are your brain cells to use the oxygen that your blood carries. You are well aware of what happens to any air-breathing creature when it is deprived of oxygen. If the deprivation is lengthy enough, the organism dies. Similarly within your brain, if the oxygen starvation is long enough maintained, brain cells die. In any event, to the extent that alcohol is in the blood stream, to that extent brain cells are unable to carry on their usual work. More precisely, this is what takes place within your brain as you drink.

Gram for gram, brain tissue needs four times as much oxygen as any other body organ. We would therefore suspect that as the oxygen attrition (starvation) alcohol imposes upon the brain increases, brain cells would suffer first and the most seriously. If the need for oxygen is the greatest in the brain compared to all other bodily organs, then any reduction in the general availability of oxygen would hit the brain first. Furthermore, within the brain itself there are differing oxygen needs. The highest levels of the brain (new brain) demand more oxygen just for survival than do lower (old brain) areas. It follows therefore that these higher levels would be the first to be affected by oxygen attrition and that the behavior patterns controlled by these levels would be the first to disappear. This is exactly what happens.

The principle that operates under such conditions is: "As the ability of brain cells to utilize oxygen is reduced, behavior patterns disappear in direct relation to their length of existence." This means that the brain maintains a kind of "last in, first out" (LIFO) inventory and, when it is placed under oxygen attrition, the first habits to be lost are the most recently acquired ones. Recall, if you will, the behavior of our experimental subjects at the cocktail party. Remember that as more alcohol was consumed there was a decreasing awareness of the need to consider the rights and privileges of the other fellow. Behavior became increasingly "I-centered" and personal wish came more and more to dominate behavior. The future (and its consequences) became nonexistent, the past was forgotten, and all that remained was a pressing demand to follow the personal inclinations inspired by the desire of the moment. The resulting behavior was foresightless, inconsiderate, and without conscience. Judgment disappeared, thoughtfulness faltered, and "what *I* want to do right now" became the order of the day. Why should this be true?

We already have said that the social inhibitions (those considerations for the rights and privileges of others) are late in developing and furthermore that we are continuously learning them throughout our lives. These, therefore, are our most recent of habits. Following our LIFO principle, we would expect that the social inhibitions would be the earliest habits to be affected as intoxication progresses. Your own observations have shown this to be the case. As we drink, we become increasingly unconcerned with what others may think.

This principle may be extended to show how it remains true. Studies tell us that we humans learn to walk efficiently at about two and one-half years of age. We learn to talk efficiently at about four and one-half. If therefore, we pour increasing amounts of alcohol into our blood streams there will come a time when our speech thickens and we have difficulty in enunciating our words clearly. With more alcohol, we begin to stagger as we walk and to have serious difficulty in going where we wish; we veer in our direction and our progress forward involves a series of "tackings." From our

LIFO principle, this is exactly what we would expect; walking is an "older" habit than talking and withstands a consequent greater oxygen attrition before it is affected.

You already know what happens to behavior under intoxicating conditions. Recall the time you attempted to "reason" with a drunk? How far did you get? Remember? None of your appeals, however cogent or based in undeniable logic had much effect, did they? Might you not just as well have saved your breath and energy? There was no appeal to reason, pure or otherwise because, you see, there was no "reason" to which you could appeal. The reasoning part of the brain was involved in a battle just to stay alive and it had no energy to spare for "thinking." Only the old brain and its "I-ness" remained.

We now can see how it is that as the new brain becomes increasingly anesthetized by alcohol in the blood stream, the old brain takes more and more control of our behavior and our personal desire comes to dictate our reactions. However, it is a fortunate truth that our dealings with the drunken man are relatively rare. Consequently, for all practical purposes our discussion of the effect of alcohol upon behavior has been of illustrative value only. It has served to highlight some new-brain-old-brain relationships and to increase our basic understanding of how our "minds work." Nevertheless, there still is a point to be made.

Remember that alcohol attacks the highest brain levels first. The highest level of all is the cortex—that thin layer of complex nervous tissue that covers the brain itself. Within the cortex lie brain mechanisms that normally control human behavior in its finest and most you-oriented form. Under alcohol these functions cease. Therefore, alcohol decorticates the brain; alcohol knocks out cortical functioning and we have observed in some detail exactly how this occurs.

We have also described the effects of emotion upon human

behavior. Remember that under emotional conditions we again behave as though our personal body need of the moment were the only guide to our reactions. We now can say that "Emotion *functionally* decorticates the brain." Think back for a moment to our organization chart and our brief description of the functions and controls it represented. We said that when there was enough disturbance "down the line" that the man on top lost his checkreins and became essentially subservient to demands arising within lower echelons. Within the brain, this also happens when feelings run strongly. There is then so much disturbance (activity) within the old brain that all available energy is consumed and none is left to carry information "upstairs" for top management consideration. Consequently, behavioral decisions are made at the old brain level where vision cannot exceed the needs of the "I." This is an abnormal (different from the customary) condition and is maintained until the energy concentrated within the old brain is burned out. In the brain as in business—let there be enough disturbance at lower levels and normal operations cease.

When our feelings get the better of us we behave very much as we do when we are intoxicated; our behavior is directed by what we want at the moment. So, while we may have to deal with the drunk but infrequently, we come face to face with feeling every day of our interpersonal lives. If we become (as we do) increasingly activated by the personal pronoun, the "I," as our emotions heighten, then you who routinely must meet mankind in face-to-face relationships must have basic understanding of what makes people tick if you are to be patient and consequently effective. By now it should seem reasonable to you that interpersonal effectiveness is primarily a new brain function, that there is very little room for the old brain when you are dealing with people. In short, there is no place for a sensitive ego at the managerial level. No man in leadership position can afford to indulge his personal pronoun.

The reason for this statement is clear. If you want the coöperation of your fellow men (and you will say that you do), then you have your best chance of obtaining this coöperation if you keep yourself functioning at the level of your new brain. Think back for a moment. Has it not been true that every time you have permitted your old brain to get into the act, you have been in trouble afterwards? "Trouble" like having to go back to a man and apologize; like finding your group in the "sulks" for a while; like worrying about the reaction of your boss when the event comes to his ears; like wondering what the other person may do to "get even"; like remorse for the fool you have been to let your feelings get the better of you?

Are these not reasons enough to do what you can to keep your thoughtful judgment high and your personal feelings low in your human equation? The fact is that, by and large, interpersonal problems cannot be resolved at the old brain level. Consequently, the leader must keep his behavior governed by the vision of his new brain.

However, this is not a simple matter of deciding. It is not an easy thing to keep our new brain in control. As with any decision we may make, a price is involved. Just to "decide" to keep thinking more and feeling less is but a small fraction of the task. The major aspect lies in the price you will have to pay for the decision itself and it is this price that should give you pause. Use your new brain at this point and consider the implications before you make your decision so that you are not dismayed when the bill is presented—and it will be presented; on this you may depend.

Let us take a look at the price asked by new brain control. You will recall (I hope) that emotion is a bodily preparation for *action;* that emotion prepares you for violent and enduring physical activity when, as your old brain sees things, your integrity is threatened. Consequently, when your personal feelings become involved, energy for this action is mobilized. If you cannot fight or flee (and thereby burn this mobilized energy) where may it go? What may it do? It is there, within your body, ready for expenditure but under the conditions of a social living, there is no acceptable relief for it. What happens?

You know very well what happens. You stew about, your ulcer "kicks up" again, your blood pressure hammers in your ears, your migraines return, once more you "can't sleep," you look for the unguents that relieve the rash on your skin, you reach for your antihistamine as you begin to wheeze or you do whatever you have learned to do when your psychosomatic affliction strikes. Perhaps, of course, you ventilate the energy with your "blowup" and your staff runs for cover until the storm subsides. Now this "blowup," psychosomatically speaking, is good for *you,* it relieves *your* tensions and it expends *your* mobilized energies. But, how about your people? What does it do to them? Are you therefore the kind of person who has no ulcers—you just give them to others?

The point involved here is this. For every degree of energy you expend to maintain a new brain "you orientation" over the easier old brain "I orientation" you will create a similar degree of tension. Since this tension must find release, the price you pay for new brain control lies in the accumulation of tension inevitably established. It is this tension, arising out of effort to keep our new brain dominant, that takes its toll in energy and vigor from management ranks. Most of the ailments and debilitating disorders that afflict our men of management find their sources in the conflict between personal feeling and extrapersonal demands. You need no longer wonder about the tremendous popularity of "tranquilizing" drugs—pharmaceutically, they "ventilate" the tension.

The dilemma that may be implied here is not real. It might seem as though the choice lay between behaving like a shark (in which case no tension accumulates) or in completely repressing the ego (in which case breakdown is assured). It is not a case of letting your old brain dictate or falling prey to psychosomatic illness. Despite the fact that to the extent you maintain new brain control, to that extent you create internal tension, the cause is not a hopeless one. There are things you can do; things that will release accumulated tension without violating the precept of considering the rights and privileges of the other person. There are permissible ventilating devices, acceptable safety valves, and effective escape mechanisms. Happily, you can make your own.

What do people do to escape the ravages of internal tension? Many, many things. In fact, almost as many things as there are people who put them into practice. Here are samples. Some persons paint or draw, others dance, do woodworking, run model trains or build models of other machines, lawn and garden work is popular, rug-making and tatting (by some real he-men, too), metal, leather or fabric working, conversation, cards, golf, swimming, fishing and hunting, collecting, rock and mineral working, jewelry making, mosaic work of wood, metal, fabric, stones, feathers, or butterfly wings, "escape" reading, writing poetry (strictly for personal pleasure and consumption), short stories or the "great American novel," lending helping hands to the less fortunate, literary, social, and civic group work—in fact, you name it and somebody's doing it for relaxation. You can "cry it out" or "laugh it off"— both will work. "Talk it out" with someone in whom you have confidence. Sit down and seriously "think it through." At the point of tension reduction, prayer "can move mountains" indeed. It is important for you to know and to accept the fact that you can find a permissible "something" that will work for *you*. Remember only that two standards must be met:

1. The definition of "play" must be fulfilled and play is doing something for no other reason than that you want to.
2. What you do must not interfere with the rights and privileges of others. (This precludes drink, dope, and other escapes that may bring temporary relief to *you* but serve only to bring grief to others.) [1]

Certainly the most efficient tension reducer is physical exercise. Recall, if you will, that the emotions prepare the body for *action*. Remember also that this action often cannot be taken directly or openly; commonly it must be withheld. It follows therefore that if emotion prepares us for action, then physical exercise subsequent to emotional experience is a biological answer to a biological demand. This does not mean that the instant you find your feelings aroused you must break off whatever you are doing and engage in stationary running or go for a fast walk. It means only that sometime after the emotion-arousing event, you do some exercising. If the alcoholic can wait until five o'clock for his martini, you can postpone your remedy until the evening also. Instead, therefore, of spending the evening in worried or grouchy solitariness, get out and hike; go to the "Y" and work up a sweat, do some calisthenics, mow the lawn, weed the garden, chop some wood, do whatever opportunity and state of health permit but by all means, do something. Within the limits of our twofold criteria, whatever you do will be better than doing nothing at all.

Just keep remembering that while all of us must restrain our old brain function to some degree, you who are responsible for the activities of your fellow men inevitably will find these demands in sharpest focus. Of all the frustrations your business brings to you, are there any that equal those arising from the "people problem"? Is it not in your face-to-face

[1] Information helpful at this point may be found in: A. Ostrow, *How to Enjoy Yourself*, Dutton, 1954.

dealings with your working associates that most of your turmoil arises? Is it not within this interpersonal area that your slide rule, account book, and centimeter-gram-second system fail to find solutions for you? Is it not from the human equation that tension emerges? Actually, you hardly need to be reminded of all this because these facts are brought home to you every day of your working life. The important thing is that you do something about it all, that you find your own individual way of preventing your tensions from reaching the unendurable point. This you can do, this you must do if you hope to keep your interpersonal effectiveness free from the dragging burden of worry and fear. At this point, it is quite true that "you can if you will."

So, *homo* becomes *sapiens* only to the extent that man is able to keep his new brain in control. He is not born "wise," he is born only with the potential for becoming so. The human animal at birth becomes the human being of adulthood only when the adult has learned how to keep his own ego needs minimized when he is dealing with his fellow man. When an adult has failed to subordinate his old brain to the greater vision latent within his new brain, he remains a "human animal" and, like the shark, his wish is his behavioral command. It is obvious that the odds all are against the event that this ego-centered kind of behavior will be long effective in the interpersonal field. By and large, you cannot maintain an efficient organization by asserting your will or your wish, but you can get people to do what you want them to if you keep your thinking upstairs where it rightfully belongs. Furthermore, there are ways of doing this, ways that offer you the greatest probability of success if you are willing to put them to work. The next few chapters will describe these tools in detail and, basing their effectiveness upon what is known about man's make-up, show you why they can work for you. Again, there are no guarantees, there are no panaceas, there are no easy roads; there is only the offer that with these tools you have a greater chance of obtaining the coöperation from others that you say you want.

READINGS

DeLeeuw, A. and DeLeeuw, C., *Make Your Habits Work for You*, Pelligrini, 1952.

Girard, R., "Man's Cerebrum Offers Lasting Peace, *Science News Letter*, 1948, 53; p. 184.

Herrick, C., *The Evolution of Human Nature*, University of Texas Press, 1956.

Lassek, A., *The Human Brain*, Thomas, 1957.

Linscott, R. and Stein, J. (eds.), *Why You Do What You Do*, Random House, 1956.

Mursell, J., *How to Make and Break Habits*, Lippincott, 1953.

Selye, H., *The Stress of Life*, McGraw-Hill, 1956.

Steckle, L., *Problems of Human Adjustment*, Harper, 1957.

Steiner, L., *Make the Most of Yourself*, Prentice-Hall, 1954.

The Tools of the Trade

NOW that we have spent some time on the basic nature of man, let us take a look at the ways in which we may best be able to appeal to this nature. Our assumption will be that the most efficient way to get people to behave as we wish is somehow to so arrange things that they *want* to behave in these desired ways. Consequently, if we can find means of appealing directly to the center of personal desire (the old brain), we well may anticipate that we will have the greatest possible opportunity of having our appeal answered in the behavior of the persons involved. The tools we are about to discuss are essentially highways to the old brain; roads the manager may travel that are most likely to lead him to his goal—the coöperation of his associates.

We have called these ways of obtaining coöperation by the name of "tools." This is precisely what they are because tools are defined as "instruments to accomplish certain ends." Since our "end" is the coöperation of our fellows, we should welcome such instrumentation as may be available.

However, we have said many times that any human action carries its price. These tools are no exception. You must forever keep in mind as you examine these tools with an eye toward their application that no tool is any better than the *judgment of its user*. No tool can do the job for you; at best a tool can but make it easier for you to get the job done. This implies effort and time on your part and there can be no escape from this, but you have a job to do and you can do it an easier way if you are willing to work at the task.

The fact that a tool is no better than the judgment of the user should not surprise you. Think a moment. Only you can plan, create, and devise; no tool can do these things. Supposing, as an example, that we were to select the most efficient electrician who could be found. Moreover, we equip this man with the finest set of electrician's tools that money can provide. We then send him out into the plant on his daily routine but we make just one stipulation. This is that he must carry these tools loose in a bag and, when he comes upon a job to do, he must reach into the bag and seize the first tool that comes to his hand. He then must work the job with this randomly selected instrument. Now, just as a blind pig may turn up an occasional acorn, so too would our electrician select the proper tool from time to time. But, by and large, he would be in a jam, would he not? All because, you see, we have taken his judgment away from him. The principle is that when judgment is removed, very little beyond blind chance remains.

This word "judgment" needs some discussion. As you may or may not know, your judgment is a function of your knowledge and your experience. In the absence of either of these attributes, your judgment will falter. Within your own work you have found illustrations of what can happen whenever attempts are made to base judgment upon either knowledge or experience alone. Surely you have encountered the situation where an engineer, whose knowledge is unquestioned, has come up with a design of a product that simply cannot be efficiently made in the shop? On paper, this piece may be exactly what is desired, but the absence of the experience factor in its creation makes manufacturing costs prohibitive. On the other hand, you well may know a shopman whose operating experience has been so broad that almost any job he is given to do ties in with something he has done before. Consequently, as he applies his past experience to the present demand, he always comes up with a way to meet it. However, you also know that if you ask this man for a judgment on operations that fall outside his experiential range, he may be very little better than an apprentice. For judgment to be maximally effective, both knowledge and experience must be as broad as may be possible.

Knowledge, basic to the implementation of the tools to be described, already has been provided. This knowledge centers about how we humans got to be the way we are and what happens within us as we behave. At this point, it may be helpful indeed to reread the previous chapters just to fix in your mind the knowledge of human nature that has been presented. Once this information has been made an intimate part of your knowledge inventory, you are in a position to use it in practice. This is the way you obtain experience. Experience in the application of these tools will come as a function of their practice.

When you practice, you make an effort to learn a new skill or, perhaps, to reaffirm an old one. In either case, you very well know that practice involves trial and error. When you practice, you try something: you attempt to learn how to do this thing more efficiently. In this process, you make mistakes. This you must anticipate. In fact, learning that is efficient learning (the person grows in the skill) essentially lies in the discovery of what not to do. All attempts to develop skills in rat or man within situations that made the making of error impossible have failed. When we are not permitted to make mistakes, we simply do not learn.

You must therefore expect to fall flat on your psychological face from time to time as you attempt to learn *how* to use these tools as well as *when* each one best can be applied. Recall, if you will, the first time you fastened roller skates to your shoes. Your learning of this skill involved a series of pratfalls, did it not? But, you stayed with it and ultimately you could traverse sections of sidewalk more rapidly and with less effort than you previously could walk or run the same distance. In learning to roller-skate, you demonstrated to yourself a basic principle. That is: "The only reason we learn anything is because it makes something easier to do." However, many people never push the learning process beyond this "painful" period; they become discouraged and quit. Of course, they do not learn as a consequence. Furthermore, there is a certain logic behind them. Think back. Remember, after an upset as you were ruefully rubbing your posterior, how easy it would have been to say: "Doggone it! If I hadn't put these contraptions on my feet and I had walked over here, as I knew I could, my tail wouldn't be aching now!" This is exactly right because there is no learning without a certain degree of "pain." This is the price learning experience exacts from the learner. Similarly you may find yourself saying as you practice with our tools: "Doggone it! If I hadn't listened to this psychological stuff and I had handled that guy the way I knew would work, I wouldn't be in this mess now!" Again, you will be exactly correct. At this point you are falling back upon sheer experience and denying the value of knowledge.

Right at this point, you have a decision to make and the probable price of this decision has been described for you. This decision centers about your willingness to give these tools a try. Keep in mind that if you decide to practice in them, there will be a period initially in which old tasks will be more difficult to perform as the old habit is being replaced by a new one. But then, remember how uncomfortable the next few shots felt when you changed your grip on your golf club?

Any effort you expend in your attempt to bring these tools into your habit patterns inevitably will involve error. This is as it should be. Remember that in the absence of error, no learning occurs. (Does this principle bear upon the practice of "oversupervision"?) As you are developing skill, you must expect error and backfires; it is quite conceivable that your early trials may make the situation worse. However, keep right up in the very front of your mind the conviction: "Judgment in the use of the tools will be a direct function of the extent to which the tools are practiced and the active effort made to learn from error."

We have said that these tools offer you the chance of improving your interpersonal relationships; they can increase the probability of your success with people. This statement will not be good enough for some of you. For those of you who insist upon certainty—you want to *know*—and you tend to dislike the element of chance, an increase in probability alone will not be enough. However, if you will consider this issue objectively for a bit, perhaps you may see how completely useless the search for certainty can be. In this world of ours with its continuous change and constant emergence of "new" things, we are forced to maintain an active weighing of probabilities and estimating of significances. As the ancient Greeks put it: "We cannot step into the same river twice."

If we make as objective an analysis as we may of the things and events about us, we must come to the conclusion that the only thing of which we may be certain is that ultimately we shall die. This is the only certainty that living provides. All else, everything we do, everything we believe, everything we expect is based upon a probability of occurrence. Although we behave as though some of these probabilities were certainties, the actuality remains that they are but more or less good bets. Parenthetically, it must be said that we have to behave as though probability were certainty—if we did not, we would be lost indeed. As we later shall see, there are certain articles of faith that are essential if our interpersonal effectiveness is to attain its maximum height.

Sometimes these assumptions of ours must deny the apparent "fact." As example, if you thrust a straight rod into a pool of water, the rod will appear to be bent. Actually, you see the rod as bent and this is an observable fact. However, the manner in which you may interpret this fact will be a function of your judgment (knowledge and experience) and you therefore make an assumption (that the rod is straight) not justified by observable "fact." Similarly, there always will be a certain aspect of uncertainty about any fact and "laws" defined on the basis of factual knowledge can never be absolute.

We need go nowhere beyond the havoc wrought by neucleonics upon the absolutism and irreducibility of the elements to demonstrate that any observed pattern of the events in nature continuously is changing. Hence we must anticipate that change itself is a "natural law" and must incorporate this "changingness" into our own evaluations of the things that are. At the very best, scientific or natural law is only a general principle that has been demonstrated to hold true with a rather consistently high degree of probability. Such "laws" are not universals nor are they forever inviolate. When, therefore, we say that these tools of the interpersonal trade offer only an increased probability of success with people, we ask only that you place your faith in another good bet in life, precisely as you have done with just about everything else you ever have attempted. You know, if you stop to think, that your successes have centered about those efforts in which you truly believed; that a certain degree of sheer faith always has increased your probability of achievement. Consequently, if you can develop faith in the ability of these tools to help you with your "people problem" (and this means only that you become willing to give them a fair chance), the probabilities are that your interpersonal effectiveness will be increased.

These tools, as instrumentation to your interpersonal skills, follow:

1. Control
2. Listen
3. Explain
4. Appreciate
5. Stress positives
6. Criticize gently
7. Consider the man as a person [1]

[1] J. Beckley, *Let's Be Human*, Duell, Sloan & Pearce, 1947.

Why Control?

WE BEGIN our discussion of the tools of the trade with the technique of control. We do this for the obvious reason that unless a man can hold himself under the control of his new brain, he has no chance whatsoever of putting any of the tools into practical application. Control is essential to the use of all of our tools; it is the "without which nothing" aspect of our entire program. The pertinent question is this: "If you cannot control yourself, how in the name of all that is reasonable may you expect to control the behavior of others?" It has been said that our technology embodies "all types of control except self-control." While we must admit that there is a considerable degree of truth to this statement, we must also accept as an article of faith that each one of us can do a great deal more to keep our new brain dominant than ordinarily is the case. The process of new brain dominance we now shall attempt to describe.

There are steps to control. The first of these demands self-knowledge. In the absence of reasonably accurate knowledge of yourself, how may you possibly make reasonably accurate judgments of your fellows? If you do not know how your own spectacles of prejudice are distorting your view of life and of man, how may you know how much of your judgment is a function of the way in which you view the situation and how much is a function of the objective situation itself? In the absence of self-knowledge, you cannot *know* and you will be left to reflect upon the "unreasonableness" and "unpredictability" of human nature. By and large, when we speak of such unreasonableness or unpredictability we but reflect the inevitable consequences of our ignorance about ourselves. You may be surprised when you discover how different interpersonal things appear as you compensate for your own predispositions in your human judgments.

Although adequate self-knowledge is not an easy thing to attain, it is not an extremely difficult task. It begins with your willingness to take a long and honest look at yourself. Sometime when you feel philosophical about things, look within. Look as clearly and as impersonally as you can. Ask yourself: "What kind of a person *am* I?" As answers come to you, you will greet them with mixed feelings. Some of these answers you will like, others you will dislike heartily. Be careful about these latter ones. You will find yourself saying: "Yes, I guess that sometimes I do feel that way, but—" After this "but" will come your alibi. At this point you will begin to make excuses for yourself. Try not to do this. Try to accept yourself as you find yourself to be; do not emphasize either the "good" or the "bad" as you unearth them in your make-up.

It may be helpful for you to know that *nothing* you may discover about yourself will mark you as "unusual" or "different" from mankind in general. Any feeling or thought you may possess has been felt or thought by all of us at one time or another. In fact, the probabilities are that this attitude or idea has been put into action by someone at sometime. This is true regardless of however bizarre or horrible the behavior may be. Just remember that all of us upon occasion may entertain ideas of murder, of seduction, of greed, of hatred, of avariciousness or envy. These negatives that you uncover, just like the positives, are but your membership card in the human race. So accept what you find. Matthew Arnold has described us as we commonly exist:

> And we are here as on a darkling plain
> Swept with confused alarms of struggle and flight
> Where ignorant armies clash by night.

However, he also told of the hope that self-knowledge can bring:

> Resolve to be thyself and know that he
> Who finds himself loses his misery.

The second step toward control centers about the principle of deliberate delay. Remember we have said that the new brain makes possible a period of delay between the time we become aware of a bodily need and our doing something about it. Control implies that we deliberately will impose this period of delay upon our behavior. This holding in check of the immediate response is what is meant by all of the various injunctions we are given such as: "Look before you leap," "Stop and think," "Count to ten," etc. As a matter of general practice, particularly where people are concerned, the ability to wait while your new brain considers the situation can bring you rewards quite beyond your expectations. A more adequate injunction well may be: "Before you react to a human situation, ask yourself: 'How much of my contemplated reaction is a function of how I *feel* about the situation and how much of it is a function of the situation's objective demands?'"

The third step to control emerges out of these first two. When they have been taken, the third one, personal decentralization, will be already en route. "Personal decentralization" means keeping the perpendicular pronoun, the "I," out of your interpersonal equation. This step revolves about the axis of: "It is not what *I* may want, but what is best for *us* that matters." In the comics, "What is good for General Bullmoose is good for the country" may have a certain humorous appeal, but within your organization "What is good for the company is good for me" comes much closer to approximating the facts of the matter.

President George X is an excellent example of what the lack of control can do to an otherwise healthy business. In his earlier experience he was intelligent, affable and congenial. He amassed an enviable record as a hard-hitting, persuasive, and enthusiastic sales manager. His company prospered as never before. Upon the president's death, he was elected. As president, his drive and energy became accentuated and his control slipped. Organizational check reins had been removed and he became unreasonably demanding. Where before his promotion he had been forced to listen to customers and to his associates, he now heard only that which he wanted to hear. Like many men before him, his ego grew with his job stature and he felt that he could do no wrong. His ideas became more compelling, his patience thinner, and he indulged himself in overpowering rages. In the process, heads fell. The tempo of personnel change increased and his largest plant had five managers within two years. Fear permeated the top echelon of the company and with it grew suspicion and politics. He ruled by edict born of caprice, impulse, and whim. Cover ups, misdirection, and making reports "look good" became the order of the day. Department heads who survived became masters at discovering what George wanted and then somehow giving it to him. After four years of George's leadership, the organization had deteriorated to such an extent that profits had turned to losses. Stockholders rebelled and George was forced to resign.

George illustrates the fact that genuine control comes only from within. It cannot be legislated nor yet maintained sheerly by external forces. Only you can control yourself; no lines of authority will do it for you in any realistic sense. At best such lines can but make you regret having lost control, they cannot ever build control within you. Control that *works* comes from within the person himself. The following case illustrates this fact:

A plant was in trouble. The profit margin had fallen dangerously and something had to be done. In an effort to bring productivity back, top management replaced the plant manager with an "outsider." The new manager faced a situation that would have tested Job himself. Sniping occurred from all levels, from men above who felt their judgment was being questioned and from men below who objected to the "change." In none of his behavior did the new manager show awareness of these activities. He studied his job, was unfailingly courteous, and kept his feelings to himself. However, he displayed a persistence and a determination that ultimately reduced efforts to "sidetrack" him. In many ways he "took it" but not once did his control slip. Shortly his associates discovered that nothing less than the cold hard truth would satisfy him and that once the facts were at hand his judgmen was sound. Furthermore, they found him to be fair, honest, and willing to hear whatever sides of a story needed expression. Confidence gradually spread throughout the plant, productivity increased, and the profit margin exceeded prior expectation. This took about a year. The new manager's ability to hold his feelings in check and to let unalloyed fact speak was the largest single factor in the upswing.

Personal decentralization carries with it the last step to control. If your personal pronoun generally is to be kept out of your interpersonal equation, then it must be replaced by the personal pronoun of the other fellow. This is to say that original "I-centeredness" is to be replaced by a "you-orientation." The final step to control thereby involves a consideration of the needs of the other person rather than an emphasis upon what *you* feel that *you* want. General Robert E. Lee, at the christening of a child of a friend, said: "Teach him to deny himself."

The tool of control also helps us humans to think in terms of the facts as they exist rather than in terms of the "facts" as we would like them to be. The French equivalent of our F.B.I. has a motto to the effect: "The eye sees what it looks for but it looks for that which is already in the mind." Kant said it this way: "We see things not as they are but as *we* are." To consider matters in terms of their factual content with as little of ourselves projecting into them as may be possible, three rational steps are essential:

1. *Knowledge* of the existing facts.
2. *Recognition* as facts.
3. *Acceptance* as facts.

In general, most of us take the first step with some ease. We *know* that a fact exists but we often behave as though it did not. This happens because we neither recognize the stubborn nature of facts nor are we willing to accept the fact that exists. You may have experienced this situation in dramatic form when, at a deathbed, a member of the family knowing that death will occur and perhaps even recognizing its onset (pallor, coldness, coma) cannot bring himself to *accept* the fact. We generally are able to take the first step and some of us habitually take the second, but it usually is difficult for most of us to go all the way with the third. Yet, if we hope to make the maximum use of control, we must take all three.

Facts have an unfortunate habit of refusing to alter themselves to suit our desires. They remain inherently whole and insistently operative regardless of how we humans feel about them. This fact in itself constitutes a major source of human difficulty in making an easy adjustment to the demands of life. Despite our pleas and platitudes, the principle remains sound: "All the wish in the world will not change a fact." When we must behave in a world of practical reality in which we daily must somehow get something accomplished we simply cannot afford to try to live in a world of "what ought to be." Either we adapt our behavior to the things that are or we find ourselves in a never-never land of wishfulness and regret. However, many of these difficulties are avoided when, as a formula for down to earth living, we accept the statement: "No ideal is quite so good as a fact."

Ideals are the things that should be; facts are the things that are. Whenever the two historically have come into conflict, the fact has won. Test this if you wish any time it has occurred in man's history; you will discover the answer for yourself. Consider the Volstead Act as an example. This legislative action embodied the conflict between ideal and fact in as pure a form as we may find. Keeping our value judgments out of the picture (judgment centering about which action, adoption or repeal, was *right*), there can be no doubt but that the human insistence upon the personal right to drink (the fact) won out. However, let us look at a situation in which ideal (as personal desire) and fact (as objective situation) come into conflict within the person and let us see what it does to us when this occurs.

Once more we need some perspective to highlight our understanding. Can you remember (or have you heard about) the old days when the foreman was a king? Before the national advent of unions, it was standard practice for the foreman to possess the right to hire, to fire, and to operate his area as he best saw fit. The only criteria was that the work be gotten out. As a consequence, the foreman was indeed emperor of all he surveyed and woe betide the workingman who challenged this right. It was literally true that if the foreman did not like the way a man had his hair cut, the man had the option of adapting his hair style to the foreman's wishes or of finding himself another job.

Under these conditions, therefore, let us postulate a foreman who, for one reason or another, needs personal power to maintain his own feelings of adequacy and worthwhileness.

Possibly this is because he is a mouse at home and when his wife says "Jump!" his only reply is: "How high, dear?" In any event, he has a need for power and this need is met during his day of work with his gang. What he elects to say becomes law and, so long as productivity is satisfactory, he is answerable only to himself.

However, something happens. One night ballots are cast and the next day the union is in the shop. Our foreman knows that this fact exists but he neither recognizes the union as a fact nor accepts it as such. So, he comes to work and in his usual fashion orders out the work and says who is to do what. To this, one of his men says: "You know something, boss-man, I'm not going to do it and just how do you figure to make me?" The probabilities are that our foreman, meeting this denial of deep personal need, becomes somewhat disturbed, in fact we may say that he gets furious. But what does getting mad at the fact do for him? It only makes matters worse, of course. He discovers, in rather short order, that anger as a mode of solution simply does not work and he learns not to let his feelings show. This costs him a price in tension. In order to identify ourselves with the feelings our foreman experiences, let us ask this question: "Have you ever been angry in a situation where it just wasn't smart to show it?" Furthermore: "How did you feel inside?" "Would the word 'tension' describe this feeling?"

We have here an illustration of one of the psychological booby traps into which we humans commonly fall whenever our personal desires bring us into headlong conflict with a fact. Moreover, this process illustrates a common denominator in human breakdown. It describes what is called the "vicious circle of maladjustment" and, since maladjustment means out-of-alignment, it follows that when we get out of line with facts, we are maladjusted—like it or not. We can diagram this circular reaction as follows:

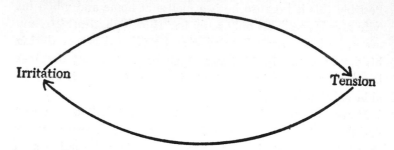

Going back to our foreman illustration, we may reasonably assume that the frustration of a personal need irritates him and since this irritation cannot be expressed, it results in internal tension. In addition, it is quite reasonable to assume that the tension itself may feed back upon and intensify the original irritation. In this manner we humans embark upon a psychological carrousel from which we emerge with only dizziness to show for our efforts. Once this vicious circle begins it does not stop until something is done to remove the irritant or to reduce its irritating effects. Since facts are exceedingly stubborn things, the removal of the irritant itself is a well-nigh impossible task. Consequently, the only hope lies in somehow reducing or removing the irritating effects of the fact. This leads us to our principle: "You cannot change a fact, you can only change your attitude toward it." This means that when you find yourself confronted with a factual situation and you are disturbed by this, your only hope is to change yourself. Basic human nature is this kind of a factual situation and, if mankind disturbs you, remember that since you are not going to change people very much, it will be infinitely easier for you to change your feelings about them.

The tool of control is helpful at this point. If when you are faced with a decision that involves people (and what decisions do not?), you will do some thinking to ferret out the odds and predict the price *before* you make your decision, you have a chance of preventing the vicious circle from beginning. In point of fact, it is much, much easier to prevent this process from starting than it is to stop it once it has begun. Furthermore, your example of thoughtful consideration before action will stand as the finest of guideposts for your people. It is a fact that your people, whether you wish it or not, will tend strongly to model their behavior on the job after yours. Unless you can show them the way, how may you expect them to find proper procedures alone? Control therefore offers two expectancies:

1. It can prevent the vicious circle from beginning.
2. It serves as a model for your people.

In addition, control can help you to avoid the Six Mistakes of Man that were described by Cicero some 66 years before the birth of Christ. These human errors are:

1. Believing that individual advancement is made by crushing others.
2. Tending to worry about things that cannot be changed or corrected.
3. Insisting that a thing is impossible because we cannot accomplish it.
4. Refusing to set aside sheerly personal preferences.
5. Neglecting the development and refinement of the mind; not acquiring the habit of reading and study.
6. Attempting to compel others to believe and to live as we do.

At this point it may be helpful to diagram the differences between decisions made on the basis of thought and decisions made on the basis of feeling. We can illustrate the decrease in accuracy that occurs when we follow our usual "thinking" practices. These practices, in diagrammatic form appear below:

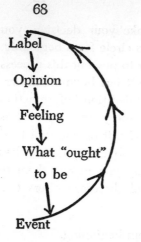

Label

Opinion

Feeling

What "ought" to be

Event

Decision is observer determined, consequently accuracy is minimal. The "thinker" looks for similarities and, when he believes that he has found them, he *acts*. The whole process is a subjective one in which the internal attitudes and beliefs of the person determine the "judgment."

Usually when we experience a situation that demands decision, we first of all attempt to label it. We say: "This is a case of so-and-so." We then (in terms of our opinions and feelings about "so-and-so") classify it in the light of what we believe "ought" to be. We wind up with a decision that is a complete hybrid and one that has little representation in the world of reality. We have attempted to warp the facts to fit our predispositions and generally we finish the process in a state of frustrated irritation. The process by which judgment is attained in a manner more in line with the factual situation follows:

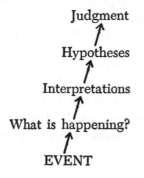

Judgment

Hypotheses

Interpretations

What is happening?

EVENT

Decision is event determined, consequently accuracy is maximal. The thinker looks for *differences* (to see how this particular event is unique) and in the process he *listens*. This practice is an objective one in which the facts of the situation determine the judgment.

In this case, the situation demanding decision is not labeled as a case of "so-and-so." Rather the question: "What may it be?" is followed by: "It could be this; it could be that; it could be another thing." Then: "It looks as though it is a— but there are these differences." "Suppose I try this for size?" During the process of the erection of hypotheses, the observer listens to his own good sense as well as to the experience and estimates of others. In this manner, the facts of the situation itself have a chance of being heard (at least they have a chance of emerging) and can be seen for what they actually are without the hampering and disguising effects of sheer opinion and belief. If nothing else is gained through this practice, the insidious beguilement in: "Dammit! It *ought* to be *this* way!" can be avoided.

Remember, however, that as you seek to hold yourself under the control of your new brain, you will build tension within yourself. Think back to our earlier discussion of this process and of the safety valves that can be developed to drain the tension away so that it does not accumulate and make difficulties for you ("How Homo Becomes Sapiens"). Since internal tension is the price you must pay for control, it is essential that you develop some kind of acceptable ventilating device. The option to this can be a psychosomatic flare-up of some kind. It follows, therefore, that if you are not willing to pay the price, do not attempt to use the tool.

Why Listen?

NATURE intended that man should be a listening organism. Toward that end we are equipped with a set of ears; nature gave us two ears and supplied us with but one mouth. A reasonable deduction from this proportion would be that we have been designed to listen twice as easily as we speak. In characteristic fashion, however, we humans have reversed this natural relationship to the point where listening is in danger of becoming a lost skill. We are a verbal people and we already have been accused of talking too much and of saying too little. This may be especially true of us humans when we find ourselves in leadership positions. In our effort to get the job done we easily deny this natural relationship between two ears and one mouth. As a consequence, the first principle in effective listening would seem to be: "Keep your big mouth shut!"

This is an easy thing to say but difficult to put into practice. The principle becomes particularly hard to apply when we, as managers, not only know what a man is going to say but are also aware of what our answer will be even before his question may be posed. In the light of practical reality the question comes to mind: "Why should special effort be made to listen when, by and large, the problem is familiar and the answer obvious—at least to *me?*"

Despite the ease with which superficial reactions to this question may arise in consciousness, there is no quick, nor yet easy, answer. You may recall our earlier reference to judgment and to the functions of which it is born. Any answer to the question: "Why listen?" must be a judged one; a solution will not be found through a quick survey over the top of your intellect. Most certainly there are situations in which you should listen and listen well indeed. Similarly, there are situations in which you should not listen at all, situations that only prompt and incisive action will resolve. Which may be which? Nobody can answer this question for you; only you and your good judgment can decide. This is a general truth that applies to each of our tools. There will be occasion where an apparently applicable instrument should not be applied and there will be times when none of them will help you; there are no "universal techniques" when you are working with people. As we have said before, these tools but increase the probability of your success in interpersonal areas. They will solve no problems for you, but judiciously utilized, they offer the chance of enabling you to solve the people-problem more effectively.

As a consequence of these facts you listen when, in your judgment, listening itself will be of assistance in making the problem solution more ready and efficient. Beyond this general principle (which can be applied to every tool we shall discuss) no one can advise you. This is why we have said that skill in the application of these tools is a resultant of practice and experience, that you will not find this skill within the spoken or written words of another person, however "expert" his status. It is therefore unfortunately true that these tools should be applied whenever their application will be helpful and at no other time. If this generalization seems altogether too vague to you, consider the possibility that you are more interested in quick answers than you are in real solutions. If you are reasonably honest with yourself, you will realize that there is little of the worthwhile that is readily available to us without effort.

In point of fact, effective listening is not an easy process in itself. It takes intent and continuous effort; it is not a thing that is automatically accomplished. Listening is hard work and possibly this is another reason why most of us do so little of it. Nor is this the entire story. A great deal of confusion arises because of the fact that much of what appears to be "listening" is not listening at all. There are, you see, two distinct kinds of listening:

1. Passive listening (you *look* as though you are listening but actually you are not).
2. Active listening (you look as though you are listening and you *are*.).

Of these, the by far more popular type is the first one. Passive listening passes for attentiveness much more commonly than most of us would care to admit. Think of the many times you do it. You come home from the job and it has been one of those days that seems to spawn problems itself. Little has gone as it should and you have "had it" all the way. As you enter the house your wife begins to talk. From the bits and snippets that you hear, you gather that she was wearing her exclusive model hat and met a neighbor lady with an identical hat on. This has disturbed her and she wants to talk about it. So, immersed in your own difficulties as you are, you "listen" but you really hear very little the good woman is saying. However, you are reasonably smart and at what seems to you to be proper spots, you murmur: "Tsk, tsk," "That's a shame," "Too bad," and so on. You are not listening, you are only pretending to do so.

Or, recall your school days. Consider the number of times when some unfortunate teacher was trying diligently to impart knowledge while you, although gazing intently into her eyes, actually were on the playground, the athletic field, at a dance, or on a date. Sometimes you were yet more tricky. Under these conditions you would occasionally pull yourself back from your never-never land, pick up a thread of the lecture, and ask a question. Having done so, you would drift off once more until the time came for you to ask another question. The probabilities are that you fooled teacher but good. You probably obtained the reputation (at least in her thinking) of being an "interested student." But you know, you could have been caught. All teacher had to do, with no change in inflection or tone, was to say: "In all my experience, this is perhaps the largest assembly of morons I ever have had to face." In the brief instant before the horrified gasps registered on your faraway consciousness, you would have maintained your expression of beatific interest—just long enough for teacher to have trapped you within your wonderland.

Passive listening is the easy way. In order to listen actively— and, of course, effectively—you must put effort into the process. This you do every time your judgment tells you that active listening is indicated. Usually you will discover that these times occur in situations where it is "unsafe" not to listen, for one reason or another. But, to make active listening a part of your habit repertoire takes work and constant practice. Yet all of us would agree, I believe, that being aware of what is happening about us can be an extremely valuable habit. Possibly the easiest way to such awareness is the practice of active listening. It does not speak for man's "wisdom" that most of us listen so little. If you are interested in an idea of how well you listen as a matter of habit, answer the questions that follow. It will be easy for you to "beat" this "test" and so if you are in the habit of cheating at solitaire, go right ahead but do not be taken in by your own answers. However, if you are as scrupulously honest with yourself as you can be, you have a chance of estimating your habitual "listening quotient." Just answer "yes" or "no."

Do you locate yourself in the room so that you are certain you can hear clearly?

Do you listen for underlying feelings as well as words?

Do you disregard a speaker's appearance and look only to the ideas he may have to present?

Do you "pay attention"; do you look at a speaker as well as listen to what he has to say?

Do you allow for your own prejudices and feelings as you evaluate what a man has to say?

Do you keep your mind on the topic continuously and follow the train of thought being presented?

Do you try consciously to estimate the logic and the rationality of what is said?

Do you restrain yourself (you do not interrupt nor "stop listening") when you hear something you believe to be wrong?

In discussion, are you willing to let the other fellow have the last word?

Do you try to be sure that you are considering the other person's viewpoint before you reply, answer or make a rebuttal?

If you have answer all of these with a confident "yes," you are a listener without peer. To the extent that "no" has been your answer, then to that extent do your listening habits need dressing up. In this dressing process, these ten questions, put in positive form, can serve you as guides as you bring your listening habits up to par.

Possibly you may be able to take a look at your listening habits another way. This will involve finding yourself among the kinds of managers described below. Keep well in mind that you probably will not be able to place yourself precisely within the range of behaviors described. This is because we seldom are either just this or that; we most always are a little of both. So, try to find the kind of person you tend to be and beware the beguiling urge to make yourself appear better than you are. With these warnings in mind, what kind of a manager are you?

1. Usually busy when a subordinate wants to see you.
2. Usually see the subordinate but talk on the phone, let others come into the office, and generally keep interrupting the requested conference.
3. Shuffle papers, make notes, check correspondence, and otherwise demonstrate passive listening.
4. Listen only until you get the "drift" and then give your decision. You don't like to waste time with nonessentials.
5. Tell the man that he has "X number of minutes" and hold a stop watch on him. Your time is valuable.
6. Regardless of how busy you are or what pressures you are under, you find time for any man who wants to talk. Furthermore, you devote your full attention to him while he is in your office.

Where do you tend to fall? Is it not a fact that you can find yourself all across the board; that what you do in way of listening largely is a function of how you feel and what the demands of the moment may be? If this is not true, you are either kidding yourself or you are a frustrating man to work for. Of course, you should try to behave as item 6 describes but after all, you are human too.

I rather suspect that each of you would reply with a decisive affirmative to the question: "Do you want people to like you?" If this is true, then possibly the easiest of all ways to obtain the regard of your fellow man is to listen to him and let him know that you heard! Too often, when it comes our turn to speak (or when we preëmpt our turn), we talk as though practically nothing had been said since we last opened our mouths. Or, if we do recognize that the other fellow has been speaking, we adopt a "yes, but" approach that displays how very little respect we really have for his ideas. The road to acceptance by your associates is better guided by a "follow your ears" approach than by the more usual "follow your nose." In fact, this latter counsel is more likely to offend the nostrils of your fellows than it is to lead you into their hearts.

At the point of refusal to listen, some of us can become ingenious indeed. There is the technique that we can call the personal equivalent of the Iron Curtain. The "Iron Curtain Drop" occurs when we fail to listen actively. It occurs when our attitude essentially says: "My thoughts and feelings are so much more important than yours possibly could be that I simply cannot be bothered with listening."

There is a management consultant who is a perfect example of the brilliant man who overdoes the "Iron Curtain Drop." Over the years this habit has lost him more friends and more business than he has been able to gain by persistent effort and intellectual ability. On the surface of his behavior, he is clever, witty, and adaptable. For any single half hour he can be a delightful companion who shows a nice balance between listening and contributing well-selected conversational gambits. Shortly, however, he will drop the curtain. The length of time that he keeps it up will be a direct measure of your importance to him. When he releases the cord, although there is no great change in his external behavior, you somehow begin to sense a difference. You feel that contact has been lost, that somehow he no longer is "there" and that what you may say somehow has lost its significance. The man is quite incapable of developing sustained human contact in any realistic form. He has had a constant change of secretaries. Characteristically, these girls like him at first, but as they leave (after perhaps six months) they frequently say: "I just can't *stand* that man any longer!" Similarly, he obtains new clients in some abundance but he never keeps them. Underneath his veneer of joviality, he is a bitter and frustrated person.

There is, you see, a very real role for humility in effective interpersonal relations. Active listening is a form of ego-subordination that can be most helpful in obtaining the coöperation of others. Your own experience will tell you that *after* a group has had opportunity to express itself and each member feels that he has had a hearing, there is then a much better chance that the group will listen to you and will follow your suggestions. Your batting average in obtaining coöperation can go up as a direct function of your own willingness to listen.

A man, aged fifty and with some thirty years of company seniority, had advanced to a supervisory position largely through technical competence alone. He was a withdrawn, suspicious, and cynical person. He was somewhat aloof from his superiors and kept quite a distance between his subordinates and himself. His failure to advance more rapidly than had been the case was a sore point particularly since he knew that he was technically superior to some men who had been promoted past him. Management's general attitude was that little change in him could be expected. However, a new department head refused to believe that the game was lost. He began by asking the supervisor's advice, by drawing him out for ideas and by complimenting him upon his technical competence whenever this was justifiable. After a while, the supervisor asked his new department head: "If this hogwash you're giving me is true, why have I been by-passed?" The department head replied: "Do you want to tell me how you feel about what has happened around here?" Answers to this question were given in no uncertain terms. The department head obtained the full story because he listened, he drew the supervisor out, and he accepted what was said with no effort to correct, contradict, or to amplify. He closed the discussion with a simple: "I think that I now understand better how you feel." After a couple more such conferences, the supervisor began to ask for suggestions— even criticisms—and these were given him with no show of feeling except sincerity. As an outcome of this kind of active listening treatment, the supervisor literally has done an about face in terms of his interest in people, his personal warmth, and his general coöperation.

The effectiveness of humility in interpersonal situations may be illustrated by a common error in human relations. If we humans want another person to like us, we often go about obtaining this regard by trying to show the other fellow how much we care for him. In the process of demonstrating our desire for his affection, we commonly do things for him on the assumption that this will prove our interest in him and will therefore be reciprocated. The greater fools we! If you will think a moment you will see how awkwardly this places the cart before the horse.

Tap in on your personal experience for a bit. Remember how you felt when someone had done something for you, particularly something that it was going to be very difficult to repay? You then felt under some obligation to this person. Now the question is: "Did you enjoy this feeling of being under such obligation?" Most of us do not. Furthermore, think back to a time when you were able to do something for another person that you were in a unique position to do; something that was of unquestioned importance to this person and really "helped" him. After the doing of this good deed, did you not feel rather kindly toward the recipient, somewhat superior to him and, in fact, just a little "Godlike" where he was concerned? Look carefully and honestly as you search for these feelings. Is this not exactly what happened within the privacy of your own consciousness?

If it is true, therefore, that when things are done for us we are likely to harbor some submerged feelings of resentment and if it also is true that when we do something for others we like the resulting feelings, it follows, does it not, that here is a human reaction that the manager can turn toward his own increased effectiveness?

The principle becomes: "If you want a man to accept (like) you, let him do something for you!" Suppose that as a result of this you *do* feel a little resentful and suppose also that he feels himself to be a better man than you are—what do you care? Is it personal feelings or the getting of the job done that is important? Remember, there is no room for a sensitive ego within managerial ranks. Your job is to obtain the coöperation of the other person in maximum form and your personal feelings do not bear upon this assignment. How you feel is unimportant, it's what you *do* that counts. Once more, this is a price you pay for the kind of coöperation you say you want.

Active listening is a highway you can travel (if you wish) to the kinds of things the other fellow can do for you that will enlist his regard for you as a person and his acceptance of you as a leader. If you listen to your people, you will obtain clues to the kind of contribution each person can make to you and for the opportunity of making he will hold you in higher esteem. But, be careful; letting others do things for you in blind or stupid fashion will bring you nothing but grief. Remember that each of these tools will cut two ways and that the direction of the cut will be entirely a function of the efficiency of your judgment. These tools are rapiers; they are not broadswords.

As we move through these interpersonal instruments, it will become apparent to you that in human relations of the superior-subordinate type, the leader uses his new brain to appeal to the old brains of his group. If this appears to come straight from Machiavelli, let us take a look at a practical demonstration of this principle. From what you know of old brain-new brain functions, does advertising appeal to the old brain or to the new brain? Think for a moment. Are the appeals directed toward how we feel or how we think? If there still is a question in your mind, suppose we ask the experts. In 1955 Edward Bernays (the Dean of public relations men in America) edited a book with the delightfully descriptive title of *The Engineering of Consent*.[1] This book represents an attempt by prominent advertising executives to tie together the principles of social science with the techniques of advertising. In the chapter on "Strategy," while going round and

[1] E. Bernays (ed.), *The Engineering of Consent*, University of Oklahoma Press, 1955.

round with this issue, Nicholas Samstag (Director of Promotion for *Time*) quotes from Dr. Karl Menninger, as follows: "—Wishful thinking and simple hopefulness influence human behavior far more than rational intelligence. Effective advertising is therefore based upon the emotions and not upon intelligence." Could anything be more clear? Furthermore, can the manager learn from the account executive at this point? Keep in mind this question: "Would advertising appeals be directed to the old brain if such appeals did not work?"

Right at this point (because it usually is pertinent) let us point out that conflict between what "ought" to be and what actually "is" commonly breeds anger. When we humans become torn between what we believe should be and what we discover practicably to be the case, we customarily begin to get mad at the situation. This is where the furious: "Dammit! It shouldn't be this way!" reaction comes into fullest bloom. While you may recall what happens to us when a personal ideal gets in the way of a situational fact, you may also be interested in the question: "Why do people get mad?"

The answer to this can be found in a behavioral principle common to all forms of vertebrate life. This principle says: "Frustration equals aggression." This means that it is "natural" for us to become angry when we are thwarted. You can test this principle for yourself.

First of all find a gentle dog, one that has not been known to snarl or snap at a human in anger. If you have one like this at home, so much the better. Here is what you do. Sit down and call the dog to you. Then grasp him firmly by the tail and hang on. You will find the dog doing something like this: First he will attempt to pull away. When this does not work for him, he may "ask" to be released by turning to look at you, whining and whimpering in the meantime. When this is unavailing, he may turn himself in a circle and, still "asking" to be released, may nuzzle your hand with his muzzle or may actually take your hand in his mouth and bring gentle pressure to bear. Remember, however, that you are not going to let go. Oh, yes you will! You'll let go because the option will be a handful of teeth if you do not. The instant the dog's tolerance for frustration is passed, he'll bite! For the dog this is good; it gets him out of an "intolerable" situation. Such behavior may also have been "good" for Cro-Magnon man as he fought just to survive. However, we well may ask: "What role does the frustration-aggression principle play today?"

When you find yourself becoming angry at a problem you must solve and this principle is coming into play, are you not admitting defeat? Are you not already at your last line of biological defense and if this line fails, what have you left? Anger, as a mode for general problem solution, may well have had its place when we lived under the law of the fang and the claw, but where does it function under the checks and inhibitions of today? Once more, the denial of this "natural reaction" will breed tension and, likewise once more, you need to have an acceptable outlet for it.

Listening can help prevent the frustration-aggression principle from getting under way. Listening can help you to insert a period of delay between your awareness of a situation and your doing something about it, a period of delay that will give your new brain a chance to assess the conditions at the level of logic, rationality, and best probabilities. Listening can give you the time you need to bring your judgment to bear; it can give you those priceless seconds you must have if you are to *think*.

In any case, if a man has something in his heart that he feels he must say, you might as well listen because he will not really hear anything you may tell him until he has gotten what he has to say said. This you again know to be true. Have you ever been in a conversation where you had a vital contribution to make—a thing that you just *had* to say? Remember how you waited for the present speaker to draw a breath so that you could break in with your comment? Now, how much of the preceding conversation had you head? Very little, was it not, because, you see, you were not listening for words, you were listening for pauses! Furthermore, from what you know about emotion and the effects of emotional tension, do you not believe that only when this tension has been sufficiently reduced will people be able to listen and to act at the level of their new brains? When you break in too soon, it is almost inevitable that ultimately both of you will be functioning at the old brain level. At this level we find only argumentation and debate; there is little reason here. It follows, therefore, that a reasonable discussion cannot occur until both of you are using your new brains. Listening to the excited person can help to bring him up to this point. Perhaps this whole listening business has been capsuled by Sid Richardson, the Fort Worth oil colossus, who said: "You ain't learnin' nothin' when you're talkin'!"

Why Explain?

IN THE last chapter we talked about some of the problems our human tendency to listen too little and to talk too much can create for us. We now must see how this human tendency can be turned to our own advantage. Just as your ears can be effective tools in dealing with people, so too can your mouth be put to efficient application if you bring judgment into the act. Keep in mind that your judgment, and only *your* judgment, will determine whether or not these human techniques can work for you. Where explanation is concerned, however, it will be better to err on the side of overdoing it than to talk too little. As a general principle, you managers are too secretive when you communicate with your people; you tend to assume that they know more than often is the case. There is something to be said for assuming that the other fellow knows nothing about the issue when you begin to describe it to him. Nevertheless, it is about as easy to overtalk as it is to underlisten but it remains helpful to be a little on the verbal side as you describe and define a task. This is because the dangers of overcommunicating are

83

less than those that develop when too little communicating is done. The following case illustrates an unfortunate example.

Dave had been with the company ten years. This decade had been spent in the sales department, rotating from area to area as he learned the business. He then was sent to a district managed by an old employee who was nearing 70. He was just "sent" there after being asked if he would like to try his hand in the field. After six months he left the company and joined a competitive firm. This created a high degree of uncertainty and wonderment in the home office. During a discussion of what had happened, the Vice-President in charge of Sales was asked: "Did anyone tell Dave that he was the heir apparent; that he was to learn all he could from the manager because he would be expected to head the district upon the manager's anticipated retirement?" To this the VP replied: "Why, no—he should have *known* that this was our plan!"

Perhaps Dave "should have known." However, none of us can be certain about what a man should or should not know; we can only be sure that he knows when we have told him and then made certain that he has understood.

Dave's resignation cost his company the price of ten years in preparation and training, a price that need not have been paid. It could have been avoided by five minutes of explanation. The cost in both money and embarrassment resulted from an identification, in the VP's mind, of an "ideal" with a "fact." The "ideal" resided in the assumption that Dave would know he was being sent out to take over the district; the "fact" was that he did not *know* and consequently, when an offer was made that promised more rapid returns for his efforts, he took it. Explanation, as a human tool, can help you to avoid such unhappy occurrences. Think back through your own experiences and look at the number of times your failure to "spell it out" cost you in money, in time, and in friction.

Implicit in our discussion of explanation as a human tool has been the advice basic to much of the Job Instruction

Training programs. Remember? You tell a man what you plan to tell him, you then tell him, and you finally tell him what you have told him. More specifically, before you call a man on the carpet for an error, ask yourself three questions:

1. Were my instructions clear?
2. Did he understand them?
3. Did I follow up to be sure it was starting well?

If your answer to any of these questions is "no," or you are uncertain, then put yourself on the carpet because *you* goofed—your man did not.

In order to be reasonably sure that your instructions are clear, you need to do some thinking about them. Remember, the words that communicate to one man will only confuse another. Tailor your explanation to the level of understanding of the man and use terms that make sense to him. At this point the you-orientation of your new brain becomes essential. One company president put it this way: "It is my belief that for most effective communications one has to continuously place himself mentally in the other man's world. Certainly if we can't identify ourselves with the other person's frame of reference, both intellectually and emotionally, we have little chance of establishing a common ground of understanding."

There are traps in the way of the kind of human understanding this president is talking about. We sometimes believe that we are doing the thing he describes when actually we are doing something quite different. This is because the attitudes behind our behavior exist on a continuum and we often do not really know just where on the scale we actually fall. Perhaps a diagram of this condition will be helpful. In general, your explanatory behavior should be directed by the attitudes falling on the left hand side of our diagram. Unfortunately, they too often reside well to the right.

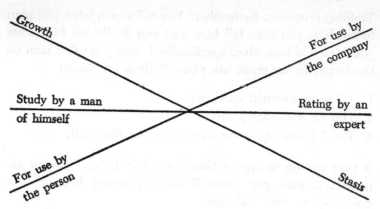

If you wish to find out whether or not your instructions have been understood as you wish them to be, all you have to do is to ask. Ask your man to tell you what he plans to do as the result of your instructions. Do not just ask him "if he understands" because he may tell you that he does when actually there are a lot of questions in his mind. But, he feels that you expect him to understand and he therefore says that he does rather than risk appearing stupid in your eyes. When you ask him to tell you how he plans to follow through, you will get an accurate picture of the situation as it appears to *him* and consequently you will *know* whether or not he has grasped the issue. There is little as futile or as frustrating as to go to a man after a foul-up has occurred with the plaintive: "But, damn-it-all, you *said* you understood!" You can find out before the act rather than fuming about afterwards, if you wish to do so. The choice is yours.

The follow-up to be sure that things are beginning well is little more than plain good sense. You are thoroughly familiar with the fact that an error made early in a program is infinitely easier to correct than the same error compounded by elapsed time. So you check, not to peer over shoulders, not to do your subordinate's work for him, and not to interfere, but only to be sure that the job is getting off to the proper start.

These three factors in clear explanation can save you a pile of grief. Make it a functional part of your habit patterns to (1) explain thoroughly, (2) check understanding, and (3) follow up.

It can be helpful to memorize Kipling's four lines:

> I keep six honest serving men.
> They taught me all I knew.
> Their names are Where and What and When,
> And Why and How and Who.

These men will serve you every bit as well as they served Kipling if you are willing to give them the opportunity. This may be particularly true of the serving man "Why." Many, many times plans go wrong just because the men involved in them do not fully understand *why* things are being done as they are. Literature at this point abounds with illustrations of increased productivity when people knew why their jobs were being done and how their work fitted into the larger scheme. As a general rule, it is always advisable to go beyond the mere "what" when you are describing expectations to your people.

In any case, the very culture in which you live requests that you ask for and earn the coöperation of your people—you cannot demand it. Your position as a leader gives you only the privilege of earning respect, it does not give you the right to it. Unfortunately, many of you in leadership positions behave as though your position itself incorporates the right to call the shots, whatever you may say your attitudes are. If you feel that such rights are yours, look into history to see what autocratic behaviors have brought to the dictator. How many of them have died in bed? Is it not an unhappy truth that dictators do not last? Autocratic leadership gets you two things: (1) resentment and (2) tension.

When you behave like the big shot boss, your people will resent it and this resentment will display itself in a thousand little ways, none of which you will be able quite to put your finger upon. Because of these vague awarenesses, you will be continuously disturbed and half-formed worries will consume you. Out of this, tension develops. In human fashion this will force you to be even more dictatorial and your particular vicious circle will be in full swing. If you doubt these statements, try it.

On the other side of the managerial fence, we find the democratic leader. He enlists support, he asks for coöperation and he tries to earn the right to lead. Democratic leadership offers two probabilities: (1) acceptance and (2) tension.

When you try to earn the right to lead, you have a chance of obtaining respect and acceptance as a leader from your subordinates. While democratic leadership offers no certainties at this point, the probabilities are as strong as any of those you treat as sure things in your everyday life. Therefore, you can bet that the thoughtful consideration that characterizes democratic leadership will obtain the coöperation you seek. However, you too will build tensions. This will be the price you will pay for the new brain you-orientation that democratic leadership demands. Because you must subordinate your feelings to the needs of the group, internal tension will result. However, tension in one form or another is an inescapable price for leadership, whatever its direction may be. The option becomes that of choosing between resentment and acceptance. Certainly the choice is obvious.

Two cultural processes work for explanation as a helpful tool within the interpersonal realm. One of these is the fact that we live in a verbal culture. There is a premium placed upon the use of words in our society. Most of the idea transmission that takes place occurs at the verbal level. Because of this, people rather expect to be talked to; the expectation that communication will be largely on the verbal level is culturally built right into most of us. This expectation you can meet or not as you wish. However, it is a natural path to understanding and certainly the one of least resistance. Talking can make your job easier for you and it will do so if only you are careful to screen your words through judgment. Furthermore, words can build a highway to understanding and growth within your people.

The therapeutic effects of full explanation have seldom been investigated. In the following case, explanation to the point of redundancy was used to save a valuable employee and motivate him to join the management team in attitude and behavior. Bill Orr is a competent, aggressive, and professionally-minded purchasing agent working for a steel fabricating concern. Early in his association with this firm, he started antagonizing other departments by his empire-building efforts, by writing critical memos when anyone came close to infringing upon his prerogatives, and by generally overdefending purchasing and undercoöperating with other departments. Drastic action seemed necessary and a new General Manager decided to (1) curtail Orr's overemphasis on purchasing and (2) try to sell him on becoming a coöperative member of the management team. Joe Jones, the new General Manager decided to make several moves that would put purchasing in its proper perspective and to fully explain each step to the balky Orr. First Jones explained at length what he considered to be the scope and responsibility of purchasing. Further, the General Manager plainly stated that he believed a purchasing agent should personally see salesmen and do considerable buying rather than delegating *all* purchasing to subordinates. He then stated that he was ready to discuss any and all questions, but he would not change his mind about how the purchasing function should be carried out. About two hours of conversation ensued wherein Orr mustered many arguments and received a full explanation of the position of the General Manager on each. In the following weeks each defection from the stated policy was brought to the attention of the General Manager. Literally dozens of hours were expended explaining to Orr why his specific actions were more or less off-beam in relation to the purchasing aim.

The General Manager made full explanation his constant practice in the crucial days when it was 50-50 whether Orr would stay or quit. And along with full explanation he consistently stated his belief that Orr could and would join the management team once he developed a more coöperative concept of purchasing. Today Orr is a coöperative and skillful purchasing agent who is operating his department with two fewer people, with fewer arguments, and with lower costs.

Actually, there is no place within supervisory or managerial ranks for the "strong silent man." Possibly during our pioneering period there was some premium to be placed on the rugged quiet individualist. By and large, these days are past and the behaviors characteristic of them also must be relegated to the limbo of things past. Certainly you can talk too much but the probabilities are that you talk too little for maximum communication.

As illustration of this point, let's go back again to the advertising field. The question is: "Is advertising repetitious?" You have only to live through radio and TV commercials to answer this. Of course advertising is repetitious. It repeats itself to the point of irritation at times. However, another question must now be answered. This one asks: "Would advertising be repetitious if repetition did not work?" The answer to this is equally obvious. Certainly in the competitive advertising area nothing is done for very long that is not functional. Repetition is advertising's stock in trade. Here again the manager can learn from the account executive. If people respond affirmatively to repetition as such, then does not the willingness to say it and say it again offer an increased probability that your communications will be more efficient?

Perhaps, however, you are one of those who prides himself on the fact that his people know where and how he stands on every issue. You speak your mind and you let them know the score. You take personal satisfaction in expressing your convictions and your people know where they stand as well. There is a question you should consider if you are this outspoken: "Do you behave in the same identical way with your boss?" If not, why not? Are you scared or just inconsistent? You are one or the other, you know, and in fact you very well may be some of both. It is quite possible that you would have been an excellent drill sergeant for Frederick the Great, but the probabilities suggest that you are a poor manager indeed.

But before we throw the baby out with the bath, let us remind ourselves that you can be a veritable mad bull, that you can behave in almost any manner and still obtain respect *if you are consistent.* So long as you treat everybody the same, subordinates, peers, and superiors alike, so long as you do this, your associates will respect you. Oh, this respect may be a bit on the grudging side: "That old hardheaded character is tough to work for but, by golly, he doesn't play any favorites!" but it is respect nevertheless.

Remember this. No matter how you say whatever you say, your words will be less important than the meaning your listener reads into them. Of course you must tailor your vocabulary to the general understanding of the people you are dealing with but what your words mean to them will be much more important than the words themselves. You must be as certain as you can that the words you use are not only within the vocabularies of your people but you must be even yet more careful to be sure that these words are interpreted as you wish them to be. In all forms of communication, the meaning that is transferred will determine the action taken— at best words are but one vehicle for meaning. If your people would say to you: "I hear what you say, but what do you mean?" your communication problems would largely be solved. Unhappily your people do not (and probably will not) do this. Consequently, only you can make reasonably certain that you are being understood. To do this, you must do more than just express your message and then ask: "Do you understand?" (inevitable answer: "Yes") or: "Are there any questions?" (inevitable answer: "No").

Unless you live in a world of your own, you will not be able to fall back upon the defense used by the Mock Turtle in *Alice in Wonderland*. When Alice questioned the meaning of the Mock Turtle's words, she was answered by: "I mean what I *say!*" You must also beware of the attitude expressed by Humpty-Dumpty in Lewis Carroll's *Through the Looking Glass*. Here, the conversation ran something as follows:

"There's glory for you," said Humpty Dumpty.
"I don't know what you mean by 'glory,' " replied Alice.
"Of course you don't—till I tell you. I meant there's 'a nice knock-down argument for you!' "
"But 'glory' doesn't mean 'a nice knock-down argument,' " Alice objected.
"When *I* use a word," Humpty Dumpty said scornfully, "it means just *what I choose it to mean*—neither more nor less."

When you have an idea that you want to get across to your people, be sure to prepare your idea for its presentation. You must decide clearly and specifically what the whole aspect of your idea may be. Look into its implications and into its future impacts as well. Be sure that you fully comprehend both the major values of your idea and its fringe details. Ask yourself: "What *are* the principle aspects of this?" "What *are* the pertinent details that inevitably will get involved?" Have the overall plan, its major parts and the pertinent details well in mind before you attempt to present the idea itself.

Once you have formulated this outline of your idea within your own mind, arrange the facts of the matter where they are likely to carry the most convincing weight. At this point in particular Kipling's Six Serving Men will assist you markedly. When your presentation structure is complete, check it for continuity, logic, completeness, and appeal. Be sure that you do not have too many details under any one heading. Remember that it is easy to swamp prospective listeners with the inclusiveness of your logic only to leave them floundering in a morass of half-submerged meanings.

Because of the danger that lurks within efforts to convey too much too quickly, be wary of asking your listeners to absorb more than they can handle conveniently. Try not to have more than five details within any one single concept. Break it down and partially digest it for your audience in advance. Keep in mind that, barring sheer intellectual insult, the easier it is for your people to absorb what you offer them, the more readily will they accept what you have to offer. How small the pieces may be will depend upon the abilities they possess to bite, chew, and swallow. Your assessment of these abilities in itself well may determine the effectiveness of your presentation. However, take one unit of idea at a time, prepare for its presentation, and be sure that each unit is mastered fully before you offer the next. This will demand time and patience of you but, if you want to obtain the maximum probability that your idea will be accepted, this is the price you must pay. If you doubt this, try some short cuts and observe carefully the backing and filling you will do later as half-grasped meanings return to haunt you.

Whenever you try to communicate ideas to your people, remember that a you-orientation is essential. Such orientation can only be attained from the level of your new brain. As a consequence, the more of your perpendicular pronoun you keep out of your behavior, the more effective you are likely to be. You must do your best to see the idea through the eyes of your people. When you can do this, your preparation and presentation will be guided by this perspective and your chances of finding acceptance mount rapidly. Keep in mind that your capacity for patience and tolerance will be tested because your success may be a partial function, at least, of the ability of the most slow-witted member of your audience to understand what you are talking about. Once more, these techniques of idea presentation will not get the idea across for you, they will only increase the probability of this. No tool, you know, is any better than the judgment of the man who is using it.

Why Appreciate?

APPRECIATION expressed for a contribution well made is one of the most powerful tools that is available to the supervisor. There is no highway to the old brain that is more open than the road of appreciation. The feeling of being wanted, of being worth while, of having done well taps into the energy resources of human action as no other device can do. The tool of appreciation can get you more of the things you say you want than a lifetime of drive and determination. Of course, if your drive and determination are leavened with the human understanding that underlies the effective application of this tool, you have it made indeed!

As an example of what this tool can do for a supervisor and also of the value of humility in interpersonal relations, read the case illustration that follows:

Here was a supervisor with 20 years of experience in handling machine press operators. He was recognized as a man who knew presses and as one who could obtain coöperation from his people. When he was given the task of setting up a press line in a new building, he had things going smoothly in short order. At this point, primarily because no one else was available, he was placed in charge of a group of 50 women in an assembly operation. He knew nothing about this assembly and he had never supervised women

95

before. Although he took the job under protest, he gave it the best he had. He got the girls together and frankly told them that he was not competent in the work they had to do. He then told them that he would do all that he could to help them, that he would play no favorites, that he would not tolerate loafing and that he would reward the well-done job. As time went by, he was very careful to show each girl that he was trying to understand her as a person. He was severe with the sloppy producer but quick to acknowledge efficiency. He showed his appreciation for good production by praise, by breaking bottlenecks, and by going all out to improve working conditions. He made very few promises but he kept those he did make. He supported his group in practical ways such as going to bat for them when machine maintenance lagged. He talked about "our gang" and about what it was doing and how well it was doing. He stressed the importance of each girl and of the group as a whole and he would not listen to petty criticism and back-biting. Within six months he and his girls almost doubled production while dissension, gripes, jealousies, and grievances were reduced. Although this supervisor used many tools to get his job done, appreciation was the one that showed marked contrast with the techniques of his predecessor—a guy who would not recognize that women were people and who couldn't be bothered to give any girl a "pat on the back."

The essence of the tool of appreciation lies in the willingness to see things through the eyes of the other fellow. We say "willingness" rather than "ability" because "willingness" is the proper word. Every single one of you can improve your ability to see things through the eyes of your working associates if you wish to do so. All you have to do is to be sure that your control is operating, that your old brain is being held under the checkreins of your new brain, and that you honestly are looking beyond your perpendicular pronoun. All these are things you can do if you are willing to work at the job. If you are not willing, you cannot do it, and it is just that simple. Of course, your alibi will be: "But, I *can't* do this!" when the truth of the matter is: "I'm not going to *try!*" While it is true indeed that some will find it more difficult than others to develop the habit of viewing things from the other fellow's standpoint, all of you can do a better job than you have done in the past.

The task at this point settles down into one of developing understanding of yourself and of the other fellow. We call this ability to see into ourselves and into the lives of the other fellow "insight." When we are able to add to self-understanding (insight), the facts of self-acceptance and self-management, we have our interpersonal relations well in hand. Check yourself—where do you fall?

The lowest level:
> You are not aware of your impact upon others. You are a bull-in-a-china-shop, foot-in-your-mouth kind of person. You talk when you should be listening.

A little better:
> Your insights are spotty because they depend upon how you feel at the moment. You demonstrate in your behavior an unpredictable mixture of diplomacy and bull-footedness.

Better yet:
> You know yourself rather well; you are aware of your strengths and weaknesses but you have no intention whatsoever of doing anything about your weaknesses. You have achieved self-understanding and self-acceptance, but where the final step of self-development is concerned, you are just plain stubborn.

Best of all:
> You have taken all three steps. You have studied yourself and you know what makes you tick. You have unearthed the facts about yourself and you have accepted the facts you have found. You have taken steps to maintain new brain control and to bring your feelings under the guidance of your judgment. In a very real sense you are master of your interpersonal fate. You are humble but not subservient; confident but not cocky; realistic but not cynical.

Be honest with yourself. Where are you on this range? When you have positioned yourself within it, you have a point at which to begin.

Now check yourself by the following questions. They will assist you in determining how accurate your rating on the steps above has been. Read these questions carefully and be sincere in the replies you give to yourself.

1. Am I aware of my own prejudices, soft spots, sensitivities, and prideful toes?
2. Am I willing to expend the effort necessary to think?
3. Do I appreciate the value of the ideas of others?
4. Can I see my own ideas in realistic perspective?
5. Am I willing to grant that ideas, convictions, and beliefs can and do change?
6. Can I listen when I do not like what I am hearing?
7. Can I ignore the appeal to stretch things a little that I may "look good"?
8. Can I be content with my own inner knowledge of a job well done without feeling strong need for external evidences?
9. Am I able to wait while plans work out?
10. Can I look adversity in the face and grin?

For every "no" you have given to these questions, you have revealed a psychological blind spot in your make-up and, if you have given very many "noes," you had better reconsider the position you assigned yourself on the "insight scale" preceding these questions. Remember, every "no" you show indicates an interpersonal area where you need to spend some effort. They are points at which your insight is slipping and where your interpersonal foot is likely to be heavy.

The values to be gained through the tool of "appreciate" are real and worth while. It is a fact that the question: "How am I doing?" is in the minds of your subordinates constantly (just as it is continuously present in your own mind), and the tool now under discussion permits you to provide answers to this universal, although usually private, query. You should not be surprised by the fact that a large majority of emotional illnesses commonly laid to "overwork" have their actual source in the behavior of the "demanding" boss who seldom gives praise for the well-done task. Positive and honest answers to the how-am-I-doing question can raise the level of subordinate morale and efficiency, as study after study has shown. Furthermore, it should not strike you as strange that this question is continuously present in the mind of the supervisor regardless of his slot in the organization chart. It is every bit the same for us humans whether we be vice-president, division manager, department head, line foreman, officeworker, or laborer. It makes no difference where we may find ourselves in the organizational scheme of things, we all want to know how effectively we are meeting our assigned tasks. When you "appreciate," you meet this universal human need.

Appreciation as a tool for obtaining coöperation must be skillfully handled and your touch must be deft. Remember that all of these techniques are rapiers rather than broadswords and that they also are two-edged. Consequently, *you* can be hurt if you are clumsy or careless. Before you attempt to put the tool into practice, ask yourself some questions:

"Is this the right time for a pat on the back?"
"Will results be better if it is done publicly or privately?"
"How can I get the tool in line with the custom and expectancy that exists within the culture of my area?"
"How does this fit in with my own past practice? Can I just 'do it,' or must I ease into it gradually?"
"What tone of voice, what expression, what behavior should I display as I do this?"
"Just how is this going to be helpful to the man and to me?"
"Will the impact of this bear upon future production or is it only a stopgap for the present?"
"If I do this now, to what am I committing myself tomorrow?"
"Do I know the man well enough and understand his reactions well enough to do this?"

You must sensitize yourself to the needs of the other fellow. Now this is not as difficult as it may appear. Ask yourself: "Are there any rewards like: (1) recognition, (2) encouragement, and (3) praise, when you know you have earned them?" To this question it is not uncommon to receive the hard-boiled answer: "Shove that stuff! Give me shorter hours and more money and you can have this psychological crap!" But I wonder if this really is what such a respondent means? Think a moment. Let us contrast two worlds. In one of these you can paper any room of your house with thousand-dollar bills— if such should be your desire. Furthermore, you can work as long or as little as you wish. But, no one knows you are alive! Nobody, but *nobody*, speaks to you, wishes you well or even acknowledges that you exist. Contrast this existence with your present life, with your present job, the pittance it brings you and all the headaches it involves. Which would you choose? Before your old brain dictates a quick answer, think some more. Do you know what is the most severe punishment that can be inflicted upon a person within our culture? Do you know what is worse than death or even solitary confinement? This most horrifying of all punishments is to be "put in Coventry." This means that although you are free to live and move about within the world of people, nobody pays any attention to you. So far as other people are concerned, you simply do not exist. Upon occasion, this punishment may be imposed upon recalcitrant members of our military academies and no man has survived it to date. Ultimately, the punished one flees to an environment where he can be a person and be recognized as somebody.

Those who make the "hard-boiled" answer do not, of course, mean what they say in any realistic sense. What they *do* mean is this: "Give me shorter hours and more money *and* the usual recognitions as a human being." To this request, we can but reply: "When you find this world, let us know. We want to come along!"

Upon occasion, people may go to fantastic extremes for no other reason than to be recognized as an individual. Many times crimes and much delinquent behavior occur primarily because the person involved wants to call attention to himself. When human beings do not receive enough personal recognition so that they can feel they are an individual person, they often may indulge in odd sorts of behavior in efforts to obtain it.

An otherwise dutiful employee came up for disciplinary action because he had "slugged" his foreman. From all that could be gathered the foreman's behavior on the day of the incident was no different from his behavior on any "typical" day in the shop. The foreman had been checking on dubious quality as he often had done in the past. At the employee's machine he had raised the usual questions and had had a poke taken at him for an answer. The employee's side of the story consisted mostly of "didn't know," "it all happened so fast," and similar evasive or confused statements. As the session ended, this man turned to the group and with some emotion asked: "Just what does a man have to do to get recognized around here?"

People want to be appreciated; people want to be *persons*. The tool of "appreciate" can help you to meet this human need. However, this tool in particular is two-edged. Improperly or clumsily used, it can cut your throat. If this tool is to be at all effective for you, you must *believe* in it. Cheap praise is the shoddiest of products, and if you attempt to use appreciation by paying lip service to it only, you will be in for trouble. You cannot "snow" your people forever. It may well be that you are smarter than any one of your group but if you think that you are more able than the combined minds of your subordinates, you're not very smart at all.

A Director of Engineering has more than his share of sheer intellectual capacity. Furthermore, if he is asked to speak on modern management procedures, he can go on for an hour about successful leadership techniques and be right on every point. There can be no question but that he "knows" what should be done. If you work for him and you bring an idea to him, he will almost submerge you in appreciation. However, if you have been with him any length of time you will be a little nauseated by it all. Because you will know that the instant he enters the President's office to bring this idea before management, you will have ceased to exist!

As a consequence of this behavior, progressively fewer "ideas" have been coming from this Engineering Department and top management is raising questions.

In order to believe in this tool, we first must have faith in people. We have to subscribe to some articles of faith; we must believe that:

1. People have the potential to be good.
2. People want to be right guys.
3. People can achieve their goals.
4. People will respond to positive treatment.

These are articles of faith; they cannot be proved. However, there is no need to apologize for faith. Think back a moment. Remember when we were talking about the role that probability plays in our life? How it is that all of us treat probability as though it were fact? That we base our whole existence on the assumption that what at best is expectation will come true? We behave as though probability were truth! If this is not "faith," then what may it be? In a very real sense your whole life is based on faith. Faith is not something for our "Sunday" behavior nor yet a thing to be considered only in church; it is an integral fact of our existence itself.

Do you know what would happen to you if you were to lose this faith? Think a moment. Supposing you were to become completely uncertain whether or not you would be alive tomorrow, whether your plans would work out, whether the things you "take for granted" were real or whether your beliefs had any actual basis. Do you know what you would do? If you think seriously, the answer will come. You would cut your throat in one of the various ways man has devised for committing suicide. Characteristically, people kill themselves when they lose their basic beliefs. So, you need never be ashamed of "faith."

At this point, a very interesting question arises. If man can create evil (ulcers, heart attacks, high blood pressure, etc.) through hostility and fear, what good might he not build through love and trust?

Why Stress Positives?

THE stressing of positives when dealing with people is but the other side of the coin of appreciation. Both of these tools express a basic conviction that people are worth while and therefore are worth being treated as human beings. In stressing positives, the same philosophy of faith is necessary that we saw to be needful if the tool of appreciation is to be effectively used. Once again, it is essential to believe in mankind if the positives all men possess are to be useful in gaining their coöperation. After all, your job is to obtain the coöperation of your working associates. Consequently, any helpful implement that does not violate human rights and privileges has a justifiable place within your techniques. Stressing positives is one way in which you can obtain the coöperation you must have if you are to be successful in your job—that of getting people to do willingly what you want them to do.

Supposing, for one reason or another, you want a barrel full of flies. In your effort to catch these creatures, would you use sugar or vinegar? The answer, of course, is obvious. You would use sugar.

People rally around the sugar bowl just as do flies. As a consequence of this fact, your associates will be drawn toward you or repelled by you depending upon whether your behavior is expressive of sugar or vinegar respectively. Yours is the choice to make; you can be sweet or you can be sour as you may wish. But, know what you are in for, what each behavior pattern will bring to you, and then pay whatever price is most advantageous for you. Let us look at some of the implications.

Where other people are concerned, you are what you *appear* to be. Therefore, you will be paid in whatever behavioral coin you spend. No one can see a micromillimeter beneath the surface of your skin; the other fellow has only your behavior by which to make his estimate of you. You may consequently possess the most admirable of motives, the most virtuous of intentions and still be but a jug of vinegar to those about you. Only when your behavior indicates your respect and trust of your fellows may you anticipate that respect and trust will be given you in return. Like it or not, it is a fact that you *are* what your behavior toward others indicates you to be. This is why the choice is yours alone.

You and only you can be aware of how you feel. If, therefore, your feelings do not show on the surface of your behavior, they will play little part in your impact upon others. If your feelings appear easily in your behavior, then your impact upon your fellows will have all of the inconsistency and the unpredictableness that is characteristic of feeling itself. (You very well know about the inconsistency of sheer feeling. How successful are you in accounting for your swings in mood and, in general, for the ways you feel inside?)

Since feelings as such are highly personal things, they are generally best relegated to the limbo of the sheerly personal and kept out of behavior. The principle evoked at this point is: "How you feel is unimportant, it's what you *do* that counts." Right here we often encounter the alibi of the complacent and the excuse for the smug. This runs something as follows: "This is hypocrisy! Deliberately to cover one's feelings by false behavior is hypocrisy of the worst kind! *I* will have none of it!" This sounds most laudable and appears as an argument of the noblest sort. Surely only those of purest heart would present it. Of course, this is the precise frame of mind the smug and complacent wish to convey. But let us examine some facts.

To you who would see hypocrisy in behavior that is out of line with the way you feel, we have a question: "How many of us humans *always* behave as we feel?" Raise this question in as many groups as you wish and see how many affirmative answers you get. It is nonsense, of course. From its beginnings in our toilet training we are taught that we must bring our sheerly personal feelings under the control of external demands; our whole life centers about subordinating our feeling to our behavior. If this is hypocrisy, how few of us are not guilty! What you who raise it really mean is that you are much too lazy to consider behavioral change and that you really are in love with yourself as you are. After all, you know, behaving positively regardless of the way you feel is but putting to constructive use a process in which you have been trained since the time when you were very young.

It is a human fact that you are what you appear to be in the eyes of others. There is a basic principle involved here. It goes like this: "What people believe to be true *is* true for them so far as their behavior is concerned." To check this, supposing that you believe that all members of a certain racial, religious, or political group are liars and cheats. Now suppose that you were to meet a member of such a group. Would you not treat him as though he *were* a liar and a cheat? You are estimated, you are known, and you are judged by your behavior.

A young engineer, shortly after receiving his first supervisory position, asked to talk with the company psychologist. The engineer said that he was having trouble with his people and wanted to talk about it. He said: "I began to have difficulty with one man early in the game but I figured that this was but normal expectancy. Now, I'm in hot water with most of my people and I'm wondering if it is not I who am at fault?" Above the fact that this man was king-sized just to face this question and to raise it, he also was exactly right. It was his fault indeed.

This engineer was a comedian of the Ned Sparks, Buster Keaton variety. That is, he was a "deadpan." This event actually occurred. In walking past a subordinate's desk one morning he took a look at what the man was doing and, in all apparent earnestness said: "What in hell are you messing about with this for?" Later in the day, he approached this man to ask about the progress of the very job he had questioned earlier. He discovered that his man had done no more with it and there was considerable mutual embarrassment.

We talked about the need to let people know when a joke was being made and about the desirability of indicating through overt behavior what the inner intent might be. After a while of this, the engineer said: "You may have a point. A couple of days ago I had to make a talk before some of my professional colleagues. About half way through, I made a joke and nobody even smiled. I was embarrassed and because of my embarrassment I grinned. *Then,* people began to laugh!"

The moral is clear. If you want others to know how you feel, let the feeling show in your behavior, but there is no need whatsoever to let your behavior dutifully mirror each internal change in mood. At this point each of us is faced with two options: (1) Our behavior can be dictated by thought (new brain), or (2) Our behavior can be dictated by feeling (old brain).

Obviously, when we can keep our feelings *and* our behavior in line with sociably desirable goals, we have no special problem. This human situation is the ideal condition referred to in all our cultural documents where man and his behavior are discussed. But, this is an ideal condition and consequently is but rarely attained. Most of us are very well aware that in general our feelings are highly personal things and more often than not center about purely ego-centered wishes and desires. Therefore by far the most of us have to keep these feelings to ourselves and hope that they remain private. Since, however, we are judged by the ways in which we behave, it is essential that we select option number one of the two presented above. If we stay aware of our impact upon others and keep our new brain alert to the needs and privileges of the other fellow, our behavior has a chance of attracting our fellow men to us and of better assuring his coöperation. Keep in mind the words of St. Matthew: ". . . all things whatsoever ye would that men should do to you, do ye even so to them."

Underlying the application of the tool of stressing positives is the conviction that there is some good in everyone. In the same breath we must admit that in certain characters this good is deeply buried. Consequently, digging for it may not be worth while. This, however, only you and your knowledge of the person can decide. It is practical to consider that those who have buried their good too deeply for search to be worth the effort make up about 10 percent of the people you will meet. Nevertheless, this leaves the vast majority of mankind open to the positive stressing approach. The odds certainly are in your favor.

At this point, beware. It is unfortunately fairly easy for us humans to perceive the bad. Somehow or other the negatives come more readily to our minds than the positives. If you doubt this, check it by a simple experiment. Here is what to do.

Get a group together and ask them to write down all the evils, the undesirables, the bad things about our civilization. When each has completed his list, collect the papers. Now ask the same people to write down all the goods, the desirables, the fine things about our civilization. When you have both sets of judgments before you, total the number of situations described under both headings, the good and the bad. Which makes up the longer list? Which list shows the higher average number of situations per person?

Since it is easier to see negatives, you must be careful that you do not fall prey to this human tendency. A rough check on your susceptability is this. If you find among the people about you that more than 10 percent seem to be those in whom digging for the good is useless, the probabilities are that their "evil" is in *your* eyes. If this happens the place to look for the basic cause is in the nearest mirror. Just as it is easy to feel and difficult to think, so too is it easy to see negatives while positives may take more arduous search. Remember, this is not because the good really is so rare, it is only because, for one reason or another, most of us find it simpler to look for the bad.

Your expectations where people are concerned result largely from your basic attitudes toward man in general. Unfortunately, many human attitudes toward other humans can be expressed by the phrase: "I don't like that so-and-so and if I know him long enough, I'll find out why!" Compare this with the attitude characteristically expressed by Will Rogers: "I never met a man I couldn't like!"

Will Rogers was a charming person but he was no genius. In fact, while he personified Mr. Average Man, he radiated an interest in and affection for his fellows. It well may be said that he parlayed this attitude into a million bucks. It can work for you too, you know. Not that developing love for your fellow man will automatically make you a millionaire, but you may very well be surprised at the increased acceptance the attitude will obtain for you. As a general rule, if you believe that man fundamentally is a sound citizen, this attitude will reflect in your behavior and people will be attracted to you. If you believe that man basically is a jerk, this attitude also will reflect itself in what you do and others will be repelled. The choice is yours.

When you attempt to estimate your attitude, however, be very, very careful. It should not really surprise you to discover that, generally speaking, the more a person is convinced that he possesses a desirable trait, the less likely he is actually to demonstrate it in his behavior. This only means that it is unfortunately extremely easy for us humans to fool ourselves although it is not quite so simple consistently to fool the other fellow.

You can get some idea of the shape of your basic attitude toward your fellows and also a hint about how easy or difficult attitude change may be for you. In imagination, place yourself in the following situation. It is winter and the sidewalks are icy. Ahead of you, someone steps incautiously and falls flat on his fanny. This, of course, is funny; it excruciates you and you laugh so hard that you forget to watch your own footing. Consequently, the next fanny to meet the sidewalk is your own. Now, if you cannot laugh at this second pratfall, you have a sense of comic, sure enough, but you have no sense of humor and it will be difficult for you to change your attitudes.

Since attitudes predispose to behavior, the probabilities are strong that you behave according to the way you feel about things. Consequently, in a sense, managerial success is as dependent upon your internal attitudes as it is upon your external behavior. An effective manager somehow needs to achieve a balance between discontent and serenity. He must at one and the same time find an internal peace and yet be constantly alert for ways through which he can make things better. Many times the effort to attain such equilibrium strains managerial adjustment. It is possible that a quick and rough survey of your internal attitudes could be helpful right here. Read the following ten statements and answer them with either "yes" or "no."

1. People seldom take advantage of the leader who shows compassion and understanding.
2. A manager should be very considerate of the feelings of his subordinates.
3. Good supervisors benefit more from training then poor supervisors.
4. Managers should usually consult with their subordinates before acting.
5. People do not need to be supervised closely in order to show high productivity.
6. Extra credit and recognition should not be reserved for the high producer.
7. The more frequently a person's production is checked, the less likely he is to increase his productivity.
8. Subordinates frequently should be encouraged to make suggestions.
9. No manager should have absolute authority in his area of responsibility.
10. A manager should always talk over job changes with those concerned before putting the changes into effect.

For each "no" answer you have given, look into your basic attitudes about people. The facts are that each of the above statements should evoke an affirmative response if your attitudes generally are on the positive side. To the extent, therefore, that you have made negative answers, to that extent it will be difficult for you to stress positives in your interpersonal relations.

Suppose we consider these statements individually and show why positive attitudes are indicated by affirmative answers.

1. People seldom take advantage of the leader who shows compassion and understanding.

We admit at once that *some* people will take such advantage at *some* times. However, we are betting probabilities and the odds are that understanding and compassion will get you more coöperation over the long pull than they will make you a mark for the sharpshooter. Studies have shown that understanding supervisors obtain more production than do the "chew-out" experts.

2. A manager should be very considerate of the feelings of his subordinates.

Consideration does not mean weakness, softness, or fear. Nor does it mean coddling or spoon-feeding. It means only the sensitivity to and the interest in the inner needs of your fellow worker that characterizes the "you-oriented" manager. A question arises: "Should a manager be as considerate of his people as a farmer is of his horse or a machine operator of his machine?"

3. Good supervisors benefit more from training than poor supervisors.

If you think a moment, you will realize the truth in this statement. Supposing you had two groups of employees—one group has demonstrated interest, willingness to learn, and productivity, while the other group has shown interest only in "getting by." If you wished to give some presupervisory training to your people, which group would you select to be so trained? Furthermore, this statement implies that at least double effort should be spent on the "poor" supervisor if his effectiveness is to be increased.

4. Managers should usually consult with their subordinates before acting.

Of course, if you are a manager in any real sense, you rather automatically *do* this. Ask yourself: "What do you *do* when you are faced with a problem?" Is it not a fact that you talk it over with your people in your effort to "get the facts"? This is consultation. Moreover, you certainly have learned that if your subordinates are brought into a problem early in the game, they are more likely to go along with your decision about it.

5. People do not need to be supervised closely in order to show productivity.

In any functional team, each player becomes his own inspector in effect. It also is known that general (broad and people-oriented) supervision is more effective than specific (narrow and technically-oriented) supervision. The evidence indicates clearly that close supervision is associated with low productivity while general supervision is associated with high productivity.

6. Extra credit and recognition should not be reserved for the high producer.

In your actual practice you do *not* reserve extra recognition for your high producers. Many times you have given a relatively poor producer words of encouragement so that he may not become completely discouraged. While it is true that high producers should get the most credit, those who do not measure up to the top standard should also get their share.

7. The more frequently a worker's production is checked, the less likely he is to increase his productivity.

Remember how you resent what you consider to be snooping or interference? Other people feel the same way, you know. While a certain amount of checking is essential, the manager who checks rather constantly is saying to his people: "I do not trust you to perform with any adequacy" and he is admitting that he cannot delegate to any effective degree.

8. Subordinates frequently should be encouraged to make suggestions.

When your people feel free to present their own ideas about things, at least three things happen:

a. They are stimulated to find better ways.

b. A premium is placed on initiative.

c. Pride in group work is fostered.

9. No manager should have absolute authority on the job.

First of all, no man can have *absolute* authority in any area within our culture. All of us find limitations placed upon our authority by our subordinates to some degree and by superiors to a much greater degree. If you feel need for "absolute authority," you are a dictator at heart and you probably need sensations of power to bolster a basically weak self-esteem.

10. A manager should always talk over job changes with those concerned before putting the changes into effect.

You are aware of the values in explanation. Talking things

over in advance of their advent reduces antagonism and makes the road easier because of the sense of participation imparted to the group involved. Remember that it is "natural" for people to resist change—the status quo always is familiar and friendly—and hence the greater the reduction of the "shock effect" the greater the likelihood that change will be accepted.

Over and above the democratic values found in stressing positives where people are concerned, there lie some hard, practical facts. Keep in mind that the larger part of the manager's job is somehow to get the coöperation of his subordinates. You should therefore know that there are three basic ego needs resident in all human beings. These are:

1. Needs for achievement.
2. Needs for acceptance.
3. Needs for recognition.

Every man alive wants to be able to look into a mirror and say:

1. This I have done.
2. This I will do.
3. This I am.

These basic needs essentially are pipelines to the old brain. We already have seen that the way to coöperation lies in somehow getting a person to want to do what you want him to do. There is no way more effective to achieve this than to tie in your desire with his ego needs. Stressing positives can help you to align your wishes with his basic desires. You have only to discover how his inner needs express themselves in his behavior in order to make the necessary tie-in. By looking for the good in the man and hence by finding out what *he* regards as the ways to his three ego demands, you have a chance of getting information about him that will permit you to align your requests with his individual wants.

It is quite true that the manner in which these basic needs may be expressed in behavior varies almost with the individual and that therefore no two people are quite alike at this point. However, to quit because the task is complex is hardly an adequate solution. It also is true, you see, that unless you search you will never find them and if you do not find them, you will not move your man.

Why Criticize Gently?

With no tool is the need for new brain control more important than when criticism is to be used as a training device. As we shall see, the process of criticizing is a natural outlet for unventilated tension and consequently it is easy for us humans to fall into an old brain snare at this point.

First of all, let us define the situation. What is the purpose of criticism? Why do you criticize a man? Is criticism designed to be a learning experience for the criticized one or is it intended to be a way by which you may release tension? Whatever the purpose of criticism may be, if you use it as a way of relieving your personal feelings, there is nothing in this chapter for you. If, however, we can agree that criticism is a tool through which a man can be trained to do a better job, we then have a task at hand and a goal to reach.

If the intent of criticism is the learning of more effective ways, a question comes to mind. Do we humans learn most efficiently under emotional conditions or under conditions of relative calm? Put another way, where does learning take place most efficiently—within the old brain or in the new?

Do you learn the more readily when you are angry, embarrassed, and frightened or when you are calm, thinking, and purposeful? It most certainly is under the latter conditions that efficient learning occurs. If, therefore, the purpose of criticism is to help a man do the job more effectively, then surely the more rationally it may be done, the more efficient it should be.

Let's raise a question. Is there any real difference between blunt, personal criticism by an adult and a temper tantrum by a child? You are familiar with childish temper tantrums where a three-year-old, perhaps, lies on the floor, waves its arms, kicks its feet, bangs its head and screams: "I'll hold my breath and I'll turn blue and I'll die and you'll be sorry!"

In actual fact, there is very little difference between childish temper tantrums and angry personal criticism by a grownup. Both are straight old brain functions and both are sheer expressions of an outraged ego. In that both find their base in undue reverence to the perpendicular pronoun, both are equally infantile. Both of these modes of behavior are characteristic of the human who has not yet grown up. While both of them relieve internal tension, neither of them does anything but disturb the interpersonal situation within which they occur. They may well be "good" for the tension balance within the person but they are "bad" indeed for his relations with the other fellow.

Perhaps, however, you pride yourself on the fact that your people know how and where you stand on mutual issues. You let them know the score, you call things by their right names, you are open, straightforward, and direct. Fine! Frank honesty is a desirable thing in interpersonal relations. But, are you equally frank, open, and straightforward with your boss? If not, why not? Are you frightened, inconsistent or both? While it is a horrible thought, it *may* be that you are blunt only

when it is "safe" to be so. At the risk of some ego-puncturing disturbance, probe into yourself at this point.

Let us repeat right now that you can be the most rhinoceroslike bull of the woods in your dealings with people and still obtain their respect if you are consistent. If you treat all people in the same blunt way both up and down the line, you will obtain their respect although you may have but little of their affection. In dealing with your fellow man, consistency is the greatest of virtues. This you could expect to be true since you are judged by your behavior.

To use criticism as a gentle tool of persuasion is a difficult task. Remember that it is easy to feel and much less easy to think. Behavior based upon old brain activity takes little effort, it comes "naturally" and hence possesses an ease of expression not shared by new brain functions. It is a physiological principle that living organisms tend to follow the line of least resistance just as do nonliving systems. As example, electric currents and fluids follow whatever path of least resistance may be open to them. So too with living creatures, man included. Generally speaking, paths of least resistance lead through the old brain. Since it is biologically natural for us to do things the easy way if we can, we are wide open to old brain blandishment when the need for criticism arises. Yet, from almost the moment of our birth we have been taught that the easy way is not necessarily the desirable way. In fact, the contrary is more often the case and, biologically speaking, we are trained to do most things the hard way.

If it is true that we humans tend to follow the line of least resistance in our everyday behavior, it also follows that we live up to the demands of our environment and no further. This is an important principle. If most of us tend to meet, but not to exceed, the demands made of us, then if more adequate behavior is desired, the demands must be increased.

Furthermore, the desired behavior must somehow be made "easier" than undesirable behavior. Criticism, properly done, is one way of defining the limits and dimensions of desired behavior; it is one way of raising the level of the demands.

Actually, about every rule for desirable conduct that has been described for us is designed to increase the demands under which we live. Our ethical, moral, and legal codes attempt to do precisely this. All of them are aimed at lifting mankind above its natural self and at making a human being out of the original human animal. The tool of criticism, therefore, in the hands of the understanding manager becomes but another force designed to increase human effectiveness and, as such, meets a human expectancy since we have been learning since toilet training at least, that there are external needs more important for our welfare than internal desires.

Intelligently utilized criticism can raise the sights that your people level on their jobs. It can assist your subordinates in holding up their heads and in doing their best. Remember that every man wants, somehow and somewhere, to maintain and to enhance his self-esteem and his feelings of worthwhileness. We humans cling to our need for self-worth; this need is close in importance to our need for life itself. Blunt and personal criticism undermines and destroys this vital force in our lives, but gentle and constructive criticism is helpful in building and bolstering it. Once more the issue boils down to: "What do you want?" Do you want to be a power *over* people or do you want to be a power *with* them? Again, the choice is yours.

In any event, whenever you must criticize a man (and of course, from time to time you must) for Heaven's sake, do it privately except for a very, very rare occasion. The insistence upon criticism privately done is not indicated by a need to spare the feelings of your people nor by an attempt to evade any public issues. It is indicated by a hard, practical fact. The

odds are strong that public criticism of a man will result in
the situation described and illustrated below.

Supposing that over the time you have been in a managerial
position, you have developed certain attachments, loyalties,
and feelings of belongingness between your people and yourself. This condition may be illustrated by the following
diagram:

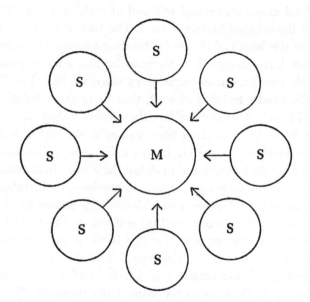

"M," Mr. Manager, represents you while the "S's" stand for
your people. The arrows running from your people to you
indicate the bands of affection and loyalty your behavior has
built for you. But now, suppose that you indulge your ego
in a public "chewing out"—what happens to these relationships? The unhappy result of such indulgence can be illustrated as follows:

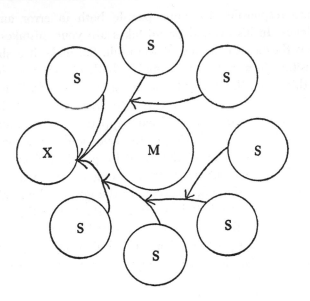

"X" is the man chewed. Notice that now the lines of loyalty veer away from you and are directed to the recipient of your public criticism. This is very likely to happen. The only exception might be a case in which "X" had tried your patience (and that of your people) to a breaking point. But, by and large, the situation will be as shown. This will be especially true if it is obvious that the majority of the "reason" for the rawhiding lies in your obvious need to get some things off your chest. This shift in affectional relations will be the gamble you take, so take it if you wish. However, take it with full knowledge in advance of the price that will be exacted. The issue comes down to this:

1. Public criticism gets you rejection.
2. Private criticism gets you growth.

When you criticize privately, keep it on a "you and I" basis. This is where it belongs because in the eyes of your boss, you are responsible for your people both in error and in excellence. In his eyes, their mistakes are your mistakes and there is thus a real sharing of the fault. So, make it a shared proposition from which presumably both of you may learn.

At this point, there may be some magic in words. The next time it becomes necessary for you to criticize a man, begin the scene with two words: "What happened?" The nature of these words implies a sharing of the error and opens the way for a mutual discussion of the event in question. This centers the whole issue about *what* went wrong rather than *who* is to blame. If learning and growth are the goals to be attained, then the "what" is infinitely more important than the "who." This interpersonal event may be opened in many ways so long as the thrust is toward a mutual sharing out of which mutual understanding may develop. As example, the session might be begun by:

"Up to this point things have been going pretty well—what happened?"

"Somehow or other we seem to have gotten off on the wrong foot—what happened?"

"I guess I wasn't very clear. What was wanted was this—what happened?"

"Communications broke down somewhere on this job—what happened?"

Keep well in mind that the *purpose* of criticism is:

1. To prevent a recurrence of the behavior.
2. To help the man learn "better ways."
3. To increase efficiency.

It is not an opportunity for the ventilation of your personal feelings.

There is, however, more behind the facade of gentle criticism than this. When your criticism is blunt and personal, you permit the man to do complete penance for his "sin." In a sense, this situation erects itself. One of your men goofs. You chew him out, but good. He made a mistake and you have made him pay fully for it. The slate is clean; the sin was committed and full penance was done. Now, where are you? In a way have you not said: "O.K. We're square. You are now free to go and sin some more!" Disregarding the feelings of resentment you undoubtedly have built in his heart, how much have you taught him; what has he learned? May he not have learned how "not to get caught the next time"? May he not have been taught how to evade a duty rather than having learned how to meet it more adequately? Punishment, you know, often only reaffirms the punished behavior—or didn't you know this? It is, nevertheless, an unfortunate fact.

In any case, let us look into some of the inner workings of human beings when a price comes due. Supposing that *you* have goofed, that you have made the grandfather of all mistakes. Shortly the word comes down that the boss wants to see you in his office. You, of course, do not have to be a mind reader to figure out what he wants of you. So, as you walk to his office, what are you doing? Are you not thinking through all the facets of your error and busy building your defenses— all the "reasons" why it was not entirely your fault, after all? By the time you get to his office, do you not have yourself well surrounded with a barrier of defense, excuse, alibi, and extenuating circumstance?

However, when you enter his office you find him sitting there, he does not look particularly angry, and after the customary greeting he asks essentially: "What happened?" What value your elaborate defense system now? What good your barriers? They crumble, do they not, and leave you defenseless. Do you know what is likely to happen at this point? You tell the truth. After all, what option is left to you? You see, by removing the need for personal defense you have a much better chance of obtaining the impersonal facts. As a manager, you recognize how important such facts can be.

The session for constructive criticism, or "corrective discipline" as it is sometimes called, is essentially a conference. Conferences are situations where two or more people get together to work out a common problem. It is an interpersonal function designed to evolve a meeting of minds. In the process of uniting varying minds into a program for mutual action, ideas are freely expressed, thoughts are openly aired, and a problem gets kicked about. All this is designed to work out a common goal so that people function together in mutual understanding. As a consequence, whatever disrupts the "togetherness" of the conference is undesirable; whatever brings the participants more closely together is good. The keynote, therefore, is mutuality, not dominance.

It will be difficult for you to leave your personal feelings, your pride, your prejudice and your boiling point out of this interpersonal situation, but if you really want your discipline to be truly corrective, you have little choice. Let us look at some practical guides to the maintenance of discipline: [1]

1. When a violation occurs, the actual problem must be investigated. The situation should be reconstructed and exactly "what happened" must be established. The important thing is to "get the facts."
2. While the action taken most certainly must "fit the crime," it should be kept in mind that the action should be corrective in nature. Discharge is not corrective (although it well may be the only option in serious cases).
3. Whatever is to be done, avoid rushing into a decision. Think about the case. Consider the man's guilt, his previous conduct, his time with the company, the surrounding circumstances, etc. Ask yourself: "What would I have done in the same situation?"
4. Talk the violation over with the man involved. See the situation through his eyes; give him his day in court. Tell him exactly what he did and why it was wrong, what you plan in the way

[1] "Maintaining Discipline: Some Practical Guides," *Supervisory Management*, April, 1957, pp. 22-28.

of discipline, why it must be so, and what will be expected of him in the future.

5. Keep a detailed record of the whole event. Be very sure that if there is a recurrence you know precisely how you dealt with the original event. If you do not have the facts recorded, you may find yourself in a jam indeed as varying memories begin to recall what happened.

In order to conduct an effective corrective discipline conference, you will need efficient verbal skills. That is, you must know how to express your ideas and how to put your thoughts into words. Think back to the chapter "Why Explain" and remember how important words are in interpersonal effectiveness. There are many things you can do to improve your verbal skills. First of all, as we have emphasized earlier in this book, you must be able to listen. Remember that you are learning nothing when you dominate the conversation. All you are doing is listening to yourself talk and you are only repeating that which already is familiar to you. You become, in essence, but a human recording and reproducing device not quite to be dignified as, "hi-fi."

Be sure that the words you use and the concepts you attempt to convey are within the range of understanding of your listener. Adapt your vocabulary to the level of the man; you will not increase his level of understanding by shouting at him. Use gestures and facial expressions as aids in getting your intent across. Stay alive, don't be a "dead pan."

Keep yourself on the pleasant side of the emotional fence. So long as understanding and sympathy highlight your thinking, there is a good chance that your new brain will stay in control. So long as your new brain is in control, there is a good chance that your entire vocabulary range will stay available to you. When your old brain takes over, your word usage becomes limited sheerly to the short, Anglo-Saxon terms. At this point you stutter, sputter, and explode.

When you talk to the man, look at him. Don't gaze off into space as though you were calling spirits from a mountaintop. Make your points directly, simply, and with as good a humor as you can muster. Keep your words pertinent to the problem at hand. Do not diverge into extraneous matters, do not reflect upon his ancestry or the legality of his birth. Keep it clean, keep it honest, keep it helpful.

Avoid flat contradictions and challenging statements. Argumentation and debate, beloved by your old brain, will not solve the problem before you. Be very careful that you do not use the critical situation as an opportunity to enjoy yourself at the man's expense. Although this will titillate your ego, it also will kill your chance of helping your man. Remember, if you want to impress a person, you first must give him a chance to impress you.

Stay away from sarcasm. Sarcasm is the tool of the little mind that happens to be equipped with a quick tongue. By and large, sarcastic comments will be funny only to you. Sarcasm has a quality peculiar to some chemical substances; it tastes differently to different tongues. While it may be sweet to you, be assured that it sounds bitter and irritating to the ear of the recipient. Sarcasm makes you feel like a hero and the other fellow like a heel. Is this what you *want?*

Criticism can be one of your most effective tools in the guidance and direction of human behavior but only you can make it so.

Why Treat a Man as a Person?

ASK any person you know whether or not we humans have the right to be treated as individuals and he may gaze at you in amazement because the belief that each of us has this right is so deep within our make-ups that it simply is taken for granted. From the time that all our cultural documents were devised, it has been explicitly stated in each of them that man is an individual person with all of the rights and privileges that go with individuality. This concept of human individualness, of individual enterprise, of individual freedom and of individual rights has been particularly stressed as our own culture has emerged and developed. The right of each of us to be treated as a person is one of our basic assumptions; it is inbred within our thinking as a very personal thing.

Beyond the fact that we always have said that we possess this right, we have no way of knowing whether or not we do. This, however, is quite unimportant because so long as we are convinced that we do have this right, we will behave as though our conviction were true. Remember: "What people believe to be true, is true for them so far as their behavior is concerned." Keep this human fact well in mind.

Remember also that about one-third of our brain is dedicated to the perpendicular pronoun and that consequently men hang on stubbornly to their self-esteem. Being recognized and treated as an individual is vitally important for us humans. The belief, therefore, that: "I have a right to be treated as a human being." is an external expression of the fundamental "I-ness" of human nature and constitutes a pipeline to the old brain that every person who must organize and direct the behavior of others is well advised to keep firmly in the front of his awareness. Every time you show in your behavior that you are aware of this right and that you recognize it as a right, you move closer to full-hearted acceptance by the person involved. There is, perhaps, no quicker road to human acceptance than the one that shows respect for this right each of us believes he possesses. For "human nature" as we know it within our culture, there is no greater appeal than that of feeling that we are a somebody and that we are recognized as such.

If you who must manage the other fellow wish to be effective in your managing, you have little option but to believe in the basic worthwhileness, goodness, and potential of man and you must do your level best to bring these characteristics to the surface of the behavior of your people. You must assist your people to hold up their heads and to do their best. Every one of your subordinates wants to maintain and to enlarge his own feeling of self-worth. When he gets the kind of leadership that permits him to do this he sets his sights higher, he expects more of himself and he gets more done as a consequence. Therefore, when the practical results of treating people as human beings are looked at objectively, the recognition of this human need becomes a hardheaded business reality.

You are aware of the current emphasis upon mental health. Belatedly we are discovering that many, many people somehow do not develop the kinds of attitudes and behavior that permit them to live easily with their fellow men. Consequently, they run afoul of our social expectations in one way or another and society protects itself by placing them under custodial care. The number of such out-of-line individuals has grown so great that our courts, our detention homes, our welfare agencies, and our institutions are overflowing. As this social problem has become jammed against our cultural nose we have begun, in typical human fashion, to take recognition of it. We are told, therefore, in brochure, newspaper, radio, and television that we "must do something about it." What we do when we attempt to "do something about it" is precisely to the point of this chapter.

The big single factor that gets a person out of line with social expectations is that he never develops or he somehow loses his feeling of self-worth. Since he is now so uncertain of his worthwhileness, he attempts to gain recognition by behavior that brings him to the attention of those whose job it is to see that the social expectations are met. The attempt then is made to bring the person back into line. This effort involves primarily a restoration of his self-esteem, because once a person believes that he *is* a person, that he amounts to something, and that he is recognized by his peers as a worthwhile individual, he is unlikely to stray too far from the social expectancy line. What is done to erect such a frame of belief is both interesting and pertinent.

Those trained in the skills of assisting a fellow man to regain full social acceptance know very well indeed that their most vital contribution to this reorienting process is their own conviction that everyone deserves acceptance and respect for what he is and for what he can become. This is to say that before a man can be helped to return to normal social living, he must be convinced that somebody believes in his ability and potential to grow and to change. Once the person develops this conviction, the first big step along the road to social adjustment has been taken. But to get this process under way, the man who is doing the leading must show in his own behavior that he possesses this faith and that he is willing to live by it. You, Mr. Manager, as the person who is doing the leading within your own group, are in precisely this position.

If in your behavior you demonstrate that you are willing consistently to stand up for your belief in the potential of mankind, this belief has a chance of permeating your entire organization. If your behavior indicates that you believe mankind to be untrustworthy, then this very attitude is what you will find within your group. By and large, your people will behave as a mirror image of their interpretation of your own attitudes. Where people are concerned, you reap exactly what you sow. If, therefore, you do not like what you see when you look at your people, take a long hard look in a mirror; there will the truth be revealed. Remember, in the eyes of your subordinates, you are what your behavior indicates you to be.

Here is a company headed for years by scientists turned administrators. As scientists, these past presidents primarily have been interested in things. As aftermath of this world-with-man-left-out attitude, uncertainties, insecurities, and suspicion became ingrained within the feelings of people regardless of a consistently sound profit picture. The current president came up through Sales and is the first nonscientist (and actually the first real human being) to head the company since its beginning. During the few years of his office, very significant things have occurred in the areas of human attitudes, feelings, and convictions. His practice is to listen, to look at all available sides of a question and to enlist the active participation of his key group in organizational decisions. Personally, he is calm, sincere, and interested in people as individuals. He tries to understand his subordinates and to tailor his demands to their particular interests and abilities. His people *feel*, deep within, that he is concerned with their welfare. His behavior toward them indicates that this is true and, over the past few years, he has proved his sincerity in the things he had done and the promises he has kept. Above the fact that never before has the company atmosphere been so wholesome, never before has the profit picture been so rosy.

If you wish to treat your people as individuals, you must look for their typifying characteristics. What about this person makes him an individual? What are his particular traits, his basic attitudes, his special sensitivities, his deep-seated needs and feelings? These are questions you must ask yourself and they set up the answers you must seek. Look, therefore, for attitudes and behavior that distinguish this man from others; look for the things that make him different. Do not look at him through the distorting lenses of your own prejudices and feelings but look at him as he is just as objectively as you can. Engrave within your consciousness: "How you feel is unimportant, it's what you do that counts."

The obvious consequence or price that you must pay if you wish to treat people as individuals is that you must come to know them as individuals. This will cut heavily into your time and your energies but pay this price you must if this tool is to be available to you. Watch your people in as many interpersonal environments as possible, observe what they *do* within as wide a variety of life situations as may be possible, and learn–from what you see. Talk with them, particularly at the chit chat level. When guards are dropped the real person often comes through. Permit them to see into you and as they are looking, gaze beyond the surface of your man; try to penetrate the walls. This you can find a challenging game, an exceedingly interesting task, and a highly rewarding one if your search turns out to be successful. Keep in mind that the more diligently you alert yourself to this human examination, the more likely are you to become skilled and efficient in its performance. Be very sure indeed that unless you *try,* you'll never make the grade; only within Anderson and Grimm do dreams inevitably come true.

As indicated in the previous paragraphs, there are two sources of human understanding:

1. You can study the outer man, observe his actions, his behavior, and how he handles himself.
2. You can dig into the inner man, ferret out his feelings, examine his attitudes, and look for his internal needs.

Both of these avenues are important, fruitful, and each complements the other. Furthermore, both are open to you although in varying degrees of difficulty. The first approach demands only an open mind and the willingness to look. The second is not as simple but you cannot ignore it just because it may be difficult.

Where your regard of the outer man is concerned, here are some keys:

1. *What is his ability to discriminate?* How effectively does he make the right decision at the right time? His discriminative ability will tell you not only how smart he may be but also how well he profits from what he observes, hears, reads, and learns. In short, it will tell you how effectively he profits from experience.
2. *How well developed are his human relation skills?* Does he know *when* to listen or to talk? Does he *show* interest in his fellow man? Is he aware of the existence of the tools we have been discussing? Are people attracted or repelled by him? How does *he* stack up as a human being?
3. *Does he possess drive, initiative, and energy?* Is he willing and able to define and follow his own course? Will he carry the ball or block for another ball carrier as the game of the moment demands? Is his drive directed and controlled or is he just an "eager beaver"?

Three cardinal externals that will help you define the kind of person you have with you are, therefore:

1. His ability to discriminate or to make the right decision at the right time.

2. His skills with people. These include his ability to stimulate, to sell, to interest, to understand, and to coöperate with others in a friendly and comfortable manner.
3. His drive, his initiative, his energy, and his determination to get things done despite obstacles in his path.

Turning from surface manifestations of individuality, let us now look at the inner man. Here our difficulties mount sharply. Many of them stem from the fact that in general we deal and think only at the behavioral level; we do not spend much time or energy digging into our inner selves or into the inner selves of others. However, if we want to understand the other fellow in any realistic way, we are forced to make the attempt.

At this juncture, you are going to succeed or fail as a direct expression of the impression your behavior makes on the other person. In a nutshell, the situation is this: If your actions themselves indicate to your people that you have faith in them, that you are interested in them, and that you believe that they are worth while, they will open themselves up to your scrutiny. However, if your actions indicate that you believe man to be untrustworthy and not really worth while, you have no chance whatsoever and you might as well quit trying. With an attitude like this latter one, you're just not going anywhere along the avenue of the inner man.

Please do not delude yourself that you are "smart" enough to see beneath the surface in the absence of any genuine faith in mankind. Take a word for it. Any human who believes that he is sufficiently competent so that he can outthink his people is living in a fool's paradise. Here's why.

Suppose you have ten men for whose productivity you are responsible. Let's assume that you actually are more intelligent than any one of them. On the face of things, it looks as though you could outthink them as a group because you are able to see more deeply and more broadly than any individual among them. But wait a moment. The surface appearance would represent the actual case *if* each one of these ten minds but duplicated the thinking of every other one. Put another way, you could outthink your group *if* each of them thought in precisely the same way. However, an instant's reflection on your part will indicate that this is not what happens. You know very well indeed that if one of these minds gets an idea on a mutual problem, another mind takes this idea and revamps it, changes it, adds to it, and in general enlarges its scope and penetration. Now a third mind comes into play and a similar process of broadening occurs. And so it goes until the concept has gone through the meshes of ten individual minds and has been subjected to the varying scrutinies and analyses of which each mind is capable. Furthermore, since any given mind may be stimulated by the action of any other, the possibilities for mutual stimulation and mutual creativeness become enormous. The problem is, you see, that you are not faced only with ten "inferior" minds, but with ten times ten *times* ten varied ways of regarding an issue. If you question this conclusion, try the course some time. Prediction: You will live to regret it!

It comes down to this: A manager with faith in himself and in his fellow man sees his people differently and more clearly than the one without this faith. The former, because of his belief, is more hopeful, more open, more positive, and more human than the cynic whose "faith" states: "Everyone is out to get his and, by all that's holy, I'm going to get mine!" He will, surely enough, but not, perhaps, quite as he anticipates.

The manager who possesses this belief in his people shows it in varied ways.

1. He maintains his faith even when he is under great personal pressure. Regardless of the stress, he is consistent with himself and with others.

2. He lives in a world of objective reality and he is a real person. (Many who profess "realism" actually are pessimists who see only the evil about them.)
3. He does not let human failure and weakness refute his conviction that man is worthwhile. He is willing to give a man the second chance.
4. When a man errs, he asks: "What does this tell me about my managership? Have I done anything wrong in this? Have I failed to do something right?" Only after some self-analysis does he set out to take corrective disciplinary measures.
5. He lives his convictions seven days a week, on the job, at home, and away from it. He is aware of the existence of sin and evil but regards these as conditions to be corrected rather than illustrations of the basic nature of man.
6. His behavior toward people and toward problems is consistent and free from conflict. In so far as he can, he trusts his people within the limits of good sense. He guides this trust by the ability of an individual subordinate to show maturity and judgment.
7. In essence, he knows his people and he treats them as human beings.

Because of these attributes, the manager with basic faith is permitted to see beneath the surface of the behavior of his people. Because they trust him, they are willing to be themselves and to open up when he is about. His faith is reciprocated in the trust and confidence that they place in him and his job becomes a whole lot easier for him. If these values make sense to you, Mr. Manager, you know how to achieve them. Remember, however, that you will not reach them through frantic scramblings within the cells of your old brain.

To do the things that will demonstrate to your people that you are the kind of person who is interested in them as individuals will be demanding upon your time and your effort. Regardless of the fact that most worthwhile things are costly in time and energy, whether or not you invest in this practice will be a direct function of what you really want. Your behavior speaks infinitely more aptly than your voice box and so, with no reference at all to what you say, your actual choice at this point will be indicated by what you do.

Perhaps you should also know that the basic ingredient in creativeness and inventiveness is effort. This holds true whether we listen to the proved creative person tell how he did what he did or whether we listen to the researcher describe the results of his investigations into this area.

Furthermore, it may be helpful to realize that the vast majority of job failures arise out of inadequacies in interpersonal relations; only a small percentage of such failure stem from technical lacks. Moreover, when subordinates are asked to describe the characteristics that make a "good" manager, they mention personal (human) traits over eight times more frequently than they refer to technical competence. Do not misunderstand. Of course, the manager must know his job; he must be able to help people who are in trouble with technical issues but he must be a human being if he hopes for real success. Of the two aspects, human and technical competence, skill in dealing with people will carry you much the further.

Let's take a few simple illustrations. Can you remember the so-called "efficiency expert"? Recall the "one best way" boys? These were the chaps who came into an organization and restructured the ways of doing a job. To keep it simple, let us suppose an assembly operation. The efficiency expert would reroute the flow of material, tightly define the movements the assembler was to make, and generally cut "lost" motion to an absolute minimum. This was efficient indeed and when instructions were followed carefully, production increased markedly. However, this approach failed, as you know. The reason for its failure lay in man's refusal to convert himself into an automaton; human resentment against living in a prescribed world caused more problems than the increased productivity made worth while. The principle involved, of course, is that when we attempt to stifle the individuality that each of us believes to be his right, we reap only resentment, unhappiness, and trouble.

Consider also the situation of the modern industrial engineer. Again to keep things simple, let us suppose a piece rate operation. The job is studied and what is accepted as a fair rate is worked out, i.e., a given number of pieces equals 100 percent productivity. The rate is then put into operation and what happens? After a time, some men may be producing at a rate of 115 percent, 125 percent, even 160 percent. What has happened? Just this. The operators work out short cuts, they find easier and quicker ways, they find procedures for "beating" the rate. This indicates that there is a tremendous mass of sheer ingenuity available within the minds of people *if* a way can be found to tap it. Think a moment—even dream a little. Supposing that each of your people regarded his job as his own business. In this business he was responsible for productivity and he took all the profit and paid for all the loss. What would happen to the output from your area? It staggers the imagination, does it not?

This, then, is the pitch. If you treat the man as an individual, you have a chance of tapping such ingenuity as he may possess; if you treat him as a number on a time card, you have no chance whatsoever. Once more the tool offers only probability and once again there is no certainty at all but you swing the odds toward yourself the instant you begin to recognize that each of your people, in his own eyes at least, is a *person* and is convinced that he has the right to be treated as such.

What to Do

IF YOU wish to get these techniques incorporated into your behavior as painlessly as possible, here's what to do.

Beginning on some one day (Monday is good because it usually begins a week of work), keep thinking of control. Plaster control right in the front of your mind; just stay continuously aware of control. Forget all the remaining six. So, for seven days just stay mindful of control both on and off the job. Do not take any special time to practice in the technique and do not put any special effort into it—just keep aware of the tool and keep thinking about it. As you go through the daily practice of your job, just stay conscious of control. It will slip from your mind from time to time; this you must expect. When you become aware that you have "forgotten" to remember it, call it back and reëstablish it in the forefront of your thinking. In essence, for one week you stay mindful of control and of control only.

At the end of this first week, you discard control and pick up listen. Now, for the next seven days, stay aware of listen. Forget control (it has had its week in prominence) and ignore the remaining five. (Their "week" is to come.) Spend a week on listen. At the end of this week, discard listen and pick up explain. Give explain its week of emphasis. At the end of this

138

period, discard it and establish appreciate in its place. In systematic fashion go through the seven tools, giving each one its regular week of prominence. At the end of the seven weeks, start the cycle all over again. If you do this religiously you will be surprised to discover: (1) how quickly these tools become part and parcel of your everyday behavior pattern, and (2) what happens to your relationships with your people as a result.

READINGS

PERSONAL

Bosselman, B., *The Troubled Mind,* Ronald, 1953.
Carnegie, D., *Don't Grow Old—Grow Up,* Dutton, 1956.
De Leeuw, A. and De Leeuw, C., *Make Your Habits Work for You,* Pellegrini, 1952.
Gleason, G., *Horizons for Older People,* Macmillan, 1956.
Hutschnecker, A., *Love and Hate in Human Nature,* Crowell, 1955.
Keller, J., *Give Us This Day,* Hanover House, 1956.
Keyes, K., *How to Develop Your Thinking Ability,* McGraw-Hill, 1950.
Laird, D., *Increasing Personal Efficiency,* Harper, 1953.
Linscott, R. and Stein, J. (eds.), *Why You Do What You Do,* Random House, 1956.
Morgan, J., *How to Keep a Sound Mind,* Macmillan, 1946.
Mursell, J., *How to Make and Break Habits,* Lippincott, 1953.
Panzer, M., *Raise Your Sights,* Prentice-Hall, 1947.
Steckle, L., *Problems of Human Adjustment,* Harper, 1957.
Steiner, L., *Make the Most of Yourself,* Prentice-Hall, 1954.
Turkel, R., *Day After Tomorrow,* Kennedy, 1956.

SUPERVISORY

Bender, J., *The Technique of Executive Leadership,* McGraw-Hill, 1950.
Bower, M. (ed.), *The Development of Executive Leadership,* Harvard University Press, 1949.
Brown, M., *Effective Supervision,* Macmillan, 1956.
Bursk, E. (ed.), *The Management Team,* Harvard University Press, 1954.

Cleeton, G., *Making Work Human,* Antioch Press, 1949.

Dooher, M. and Marting, E. (eds.), *Selection of Management Personnel,* American Management Association, 1957, Vol. I.

Fryer, D., *Developing People in Industry,* Harper, 1956.

Gardner, B. and Moore, D., *Human Relations in Industry,* Irwin, 1955.

Golden, C. and Parker, V. (eds.), *Causes of Industrial Peace,* Harper, 1955.

Simmons, H., *How to Get Ahead in Modern Business,* Prentice-Hall, 1953.

Simon, H., *Administrative Behavior,* Macmillan, 1957.

Tredgold, R., *Human Relations in Modern Industry,* International University Press, 1950.

Uris, A., *Improved Foremanship,* Macmillan, 1948.

Uris, A. and Shapin, B., *Working with People,* Macmillan, 1949.

Index

Acceptance, of self, 78-79, 97-98
  social, 88, 128-130
Action, physical, 45-46, 48, 68
  delay in, 31-33, 60, 81
Adrenal glands, 24
Advertising, 79-80, 90
Aggression, 80-81
Alcohol, *see* Intoxication
Alice in Wonderland, 92
Anger, 46, 61, 65, 80-82, 117, 125
Appreciation of subordinates, 57,
  95-103, 139
Arabs, 16 n.
Arnold, Matthew, 60
Art, prehistoric, 13
Artifacts, prehistoric, 12-14
Assembly line, 136-137
Attitudes in human relations, 4, 66,
  85-86, 109-115, 130-131
Autocratic leadership, 87-88, 111,
  113

Behavior, 4, 5, 30-31, 33-39, 44,
  105
  and anger, 46, 61, 65, 80-82, 117,
  125
  consistency in, 91, 118, 135
  and criticism, 118-119
  "I-centered," 35, 36-39, 42, 43,
  60-62, 117-119, 128
  intoxicated, 38-39, 40-44
  relation of to emotions, 105-108

"you-oriented," 38-39, 40, 43,
  60-62, 85, 88, 93,, 117-119
  See also Ego; New brain;
  Old brain; Self-preserva-
  tion
Bernays, Edward, 79
Biology, human, 12, 16-18, 21, 24-
  27, 29-33
  See also Brain
Blood pressure, 24
Blood sugar, 24, 29, 30
Body mechanism in self-preserva-
  tion, 23-27, 29-33
Brain, physiology of, 11, 27, 32-33,
  35-36, 41-44
  of shark, 31-33
  See also New brain; Old
  brain

Canary Islands, 10
Carroll, Lewis, 92
Cave man, *see* Cro-Magnon man
Certainty, 55-57
Cicero, Marcus Tullius, 67
Communication, *see* Explanation
Conference, 124
Consideration, 57, 88, 108, 112
Control, emotional, 33-39, 57, 58-
  69, 97, 138
  and criticism, 116-118, 125-126
  and tension, 45-50, 65-69, 116-
  117

141